Divide & Rule

Published in 2020 by
HERALD BOOKS, BELFAST

© Text: Herald Books, 1980
© Text: Herald Books, 2020

ISBN: 978-1-64921-979-4

Layout and design by Eddie McCabe & Seán Burns
Editorial team: Stephen Boyd, Ciaran Crossey, Kevin Henry

Special thanks for the assistance of Thomas Carmichael, Susan Fitzgerald, Cillian Gillespie,
Ann Orr and Daniel Waldron

This book is typeset in 10 on 12 point Scala

Divide & Rule

Labour and the partition of Ireland

PETER HADDEN

A HERALD BOOKS PUBLICATION
(PUBLISHING HOUSE OF THE SOCIALIST PARTY)

Peter Hadden (1950-2010)

ABOUT THE AUTHOR

Peter Hadden
1950-2010

By Stephen Boyd

Peter Hadden was born in 1950 into a Protestant family in the village of Artigarvan, near Strabane in County Tyrone. Peter's father, originally from Cork, was the local Church of Ireland rector. Peter became active in socialist politics in 1968 whilst attending Sussex University, where he joined Militant, the forerunner of the Socialist Party.

Peter worked together with leading members of Militant who visited Northern Ireland in 1969 to discuss with members of the Derry Labour Party. It was during the tumultuous events of the late 1960s that the initial forces of Militant in Ireland were established, and Peter Hadden moved back to Belfast in 1971 to work with his comrades in building a base for Marxism.

Before becoming a full-time organiser for Militant and then the Socialist Party, Peter worked briefly as a teacher, prior to working for the Northern Ireland Public Service Alliance (NIPSA), the biggest public sector union in the North. It was during his time working for NIPSA and subsequently that Peter played a central role in the establishment and then building of the union's Broad Left, in collaboration with his Militant/Socialist Party comrades in the union.

This collaboration was to have an important impact at crucial moments in Northern Irish politics, as his comrades in NIPSA were the vital catalyst in the organising of strikes by public sector workers in defence of services and against sectarian threats and murders. The Militant/Socialist Party members in NIPSA and other unions played a pivotal role in establishing a new tradition of Protestant and Catholic workers organising demonstrations and strikes in opposition to the sectarian intimidation and killing of working-class people by both loyalist and republican paramilitaries.

For Peter, the benchmark he applied for a point of programme, a demand, a slogan, a campaign, strategy or tactic was always whether it furthered the interests of the working class and working-class unity. Peter didn't just argue for the need for genuine working-class political representation. Along with his comrades, ex-members of the Northern Ireland Labour Party (NILP) and trade unionists, he founded the Labour and Trade Union Group and the Young Socialists when it became clear that the NILP was no longer capable of being a genuinely non-sectarian force. Peter also stood in the general election in 1992 and was central to the formation of the Labour Coalition, which won two seats in the Northern Ireland Forum elections in 1996.

Peter was an active campaigner against the social deprivation that capitalism inflicts on the working class. He was the driving force behind the We Won't Pay Campaign in opposition to water charges in Northern Ireland. This campaign convinced 100,0000 people to sign a pledge committing themselves to non-payment, helped make the water charges an election issue and put both the DUP and Sinn Féin under pressure not to introduce the charges.

Peter was involved in many solidarity campaigns with workers in struggle, including the firefighters of the FBU, the Chelsea Girl workers, the Montupet, Belfast airport and Visteon disputes. The impact that Peter had on workers engaged in struggle was reflected in the remarks of John Maguire, the senior shop steward in the Visteon occupation, at the celebration of Peter's life. John spoke of how it was the workers themselves and the Socialist Party which had achieved the victory; "I'll always personally be grateful for Peter and Susan and everybody in the Socialist Party for the help they gave me. Every time I go home and see my family and kids, I know who helped me at least hold onto the life I had before Visteon closed the factory".

Peter also worked closely with his comrades in the South and was active in all of their election campaigns, as well as giving invaluable advice in struggles such as the anti-bin tax campaign, and the struggle of the GAMA workers. Joe Higgins, former Socialist Party TD and MEP, said of Peter shortly after his death from cancer, "During my time in the Dáil and now Europe, I would consistently ask Peter for advice. On many occasions, it was he who armed me with a political edge when I went into the chamber to take on the Taoiseach. Peter Hadden was the giant at my shoulder for 35 years."

Peter was a founding member of the Committee for a Workers' International (CWI), which has now been renamed International Socialist Alternative, in 1974 and remained an elected member of its International Executive Committee for the rest of his life. Peter also made overseas visits on behalf of the CWI, giving important political and tactical help and advice to comrades around the world. Among other places, Peter visited Italy, Nigeria, Israel/Palestine, the Czech Republic, Greece, Australia, Scotland, Belgium and the USA. The first material to be translated for the website of the Chinese section of the CWI were some of Peter's writings on the national question.

Peter Hadden died on 5th May 2010, aged 60. Alongside his comrades in Militant and later the Socialist Party, he fought a heroic struggle against the stream to build the forces of Marxism in Ireland, North and South. Without doubt, he has added to the arsenal of Marxist theory on the national question and his analysis, and the programme, strategy and tactics he helped develop in the North have assisted International Socialist Alternative members facing similar difficulties all over the world. They are now an invaluable asset for the Irish working class, North and South, in its struggle for socialism.

Peter's writings on the national question are numerous and include *Divide and Rule - Labour and the partition of Ireland* (1980), *Beyond the Troubles* (1994), *Troubled Times - The National Question in Ireland* (1995), *Towards Division, Not Peace* (2002) and *Common History, Common Struggle* (2017, published posthumously). An archive of Peter's writings can be found online in the writers' archive of the Encyclopedia of Trotskyism.

EDITORS' NOTE

The main text of this book was written by Peter Hadden in 1980 and a later edition was produced in 1986. The content of the text has not been altered, except for minor factual and grammatical changes. We include footnotes to add further information, or to provide explanation of some terms which may not be understood by those unfamiliar with the subject matter.

Readers can find out more about the ideas and activities of the Socialist Party by contacting us at info@socialistpartyni.org.

Contents

2020 Introduction   10

1986 Introduction   27

⊕ ONE   41
Land & Capital: Class Conflict and Home Rule Before 1914

⊕ TWO   51
Labour Emerges

⊕ THREE   69
Capital Revolts

⊕ FOUR   73
Labour Unity & Reaction

⊕ FIVE   81
Socialism or Division: 1914–1921

⊕ SIX   83
Connolly & 1916

⊕ SEVEN   93
Working-Class Offensive

⊕ EIGHT   99
Labour Must Wait

⊕ NINE   105
Military Repression

⊕ TEN   109
Capitalism Means Division

⊕ APPENDIX   120

INTRODUCTION

By Kevin Henry

2020 Edition

Written by Peter Hadden forty years ago, *Divide and Rule* is a Marxist classic. The book's key argument is summed up in the first line: "The partition of Ireland was a conscious act on the part of British imperialism chiefly intended to divide the working class along sectarian lines." Fifteen years later, in Troubled Times, which the Socialist Party also intends to reprint this year, Peter Hadden said that *Divide and Rule* was written "mainly as a challenge to the simplified, romanticised picture painted by nationalists."[1] But it was also a challenge to Unionist historians and to the revisionist school of Irish history which had been in the ascendent from the early 1970s onwards. What all these schools of history have in common is that they ignore the class interests and forces which have shaped the course of Irish history.

In that regard, Peter Hadden's work stands in the tradition of those Marxists who studied the history of Ireland using a class analysis, including James Connolly, as particularly reflected in his books *The Reconquest of Ireland* and *Labour in Irish History*. These writings recognise the centrality of class division in Irish history, how the interests of both the British and Irish ruling classes shaped their actions.

This book also affirms Connolly's well-known and prophetic warning that partition would mean "a carnival of reaction both North and South". What is less commonly referenced is Connolly's logic as to why this would be the case - that it "would set back the wheels of progress, would destroy the oncoming unity of the Irish Labour movement and paralyse all advanced movements whilst it endured."[2] Crucially, however, Divide and Rule also affirms that "Labour and working-class unity were the real victims of partition. Labour alone could have averted this menace."

This idea reflects a key hallmark of the approach of Peter Hadden and the Socialist Party to the national question in Ireland, which combines a sober assessment of the balance of forces, and a preparedness to raise sharp warnings about the dangers of sectarianism, with an ultimately optimistic perspective

---

[1] *Peter Hadden, Troubled Times 1995*
https://www.marxists.org/history/etol/writers/hadden/1995/natq/ch02.html
[2] *James Connolly, Labour and the Proposed Partition of Ireland, 1914*

about the capacity of the working class to transcend sectarian division. Today, that is reflected in our slogan, "For workers' unity and socialism." The same optimism is found in *Divide and Rule*. In the introduction, Peter Hadden makes this vital point which runs like a thread through the rest of the book:

"The tactic of "divide and rule", of setting Catholic against Protestant, has again and again been used in Ireland. But history shows, not once but repeatedly, that the oppressed masses are capable of overcoming religious divisions and withstanding the attempts of the exploiters to set them apart. Unity of the oppressed has always been possible on the basis of opposition to oppression."

Leadership matters

Another important theme is the crucial role which leadership plays in the labour movement. Essentially, this approach is criticised by other historians, including those on the socialist left.

For example, Conor Kostick in his very informative book *Revolution in Ireland* and in other publications criticises *Divide and Rule* for exaggerating the import of what is described as the "criminal" decision of the labour movement not to stand in the 1918 general election. Peter Hadden argues that the policy of 'labour must wait' conceded leadership of the anti-imperialist struggle to sectarian, nationalist forces. For Kostick, it was "a missed opportunity to raise the distinct interests of the working class but it was not the kind of defeat - such as that of 1913 - that damages the fundamental structure of the working class movement."[3]

Instead, Kostick argues that "the real turning points of the period were not electoral ones but the outcomes of the incredibly radical mass movements of workers against opponents ranging from the British authorities to Irish employers and landowners."

However, these are linked. The lack of a revolutionary leadership with confidence in the capacity of the working class to take matters into their own hands had an important effect on countless struggles that did develop. As Peter Hadden argues here and the Socialist Party stresses in other publications, the period was one of revolutionary struggle, not just internationally but also in Ireland, including united struggles of the working class of the North, most notably the 1919 Belfast engineering strike. It is this movement of working people that could have transformed the situation if armed with a socialist perspective and programme.

[3.] *Conor Kostick, Revolution in Ireland, p45 & Conor Kostick, The Irish Working Class and the War of Independence, Irish Marxist Review, 2015*

As Peter Hadden put it:

"North and South one united class movement was developing during this period. What was required was a leadership which could tie together, in the minds of all the workers, the land and factory seizures in the South, the takeovers of towns such as Limerick, with the industrial muscle revealed by the Belfast working class in 1919. A common struggle against capitalist domination could have been begun."

This would have required developing a programme which would take up all the democratic demands and link them with the need for socialist change and for decisive action on the part of the workers' organisations, so that the labour movement would clearly articulate the need:

"Not just for a republic, but for a workers' republic! Not just the right to have a parliament but for a revolutionary constituent assembly which could take the factories and the land out of the hands of the speculators and profiteers and place them in the hands of the working class! Not just for rule by the "Irish people" but for rule by the Irish workers, the only class capable of solving the problems of the small farmers and all the middle strata of society. Not just for independence, but for independence from British capitalism! Not just for freedom, but for freedom from exploitation! Not just against national oppression, but for socialist internationalism including the forging of the strongest possible links with the organizations of the British working class!"

While united class struggle was developing on the industrial plane, the decision by the Labour leadership to stand aside from the 1918 general election meant this was not given national expression on the political plane at a crucial juncture. Only in Belfast did Labour field candidates. The opportunity to tie together the struggles of workers North and South was squandered. The fact that Labour broadly stood aside to make way for Sinn Féin and their vision of independence on a capitalist basis undoubtedly would have irked Protestant workers in the North and provided ammunition for the propaganda machine of the Unionist establishment. This had a definite impact on the course of subsequent events.

Similarly, Kostick takes issue with *Divide and Rule* for its criticism of Connolly's role in the 1916 Easter Rising, claiming Peter Hadden "saw only reactionary politics in the national movement."[4] These criticisms reflect a

---

[4] Conor Kostick, *James Connolly in The Bureau of Military History, Irish Marxist Review,* 2013

misinterpretation of the analysis in *Divide and Rule*. Peter Hadden uses Connolly's own description of the nationalist leaders as "the open enemies or the treacherous friends of the working class" to highlight why he believed it was a mistake for Connolly to take part in the Easter Rising in the manner in which he did, without drawing a clear line of demarcation between the nationalist involved and the socialist, working class forces of the Irish Citizens' Army. He also, like Lenin, outlines why the Rising was premature.

However, Peter Hadden is sympathetic and understanding towards Connolly's desire to strike a blow against imperialism. He explains that Connolly's participation in the Rising was born out of frustration with the lack of working-class resistance to the First World War, largely as a result of capitulation of the leadership of the Second International, the majority of whom lined up in support of their own ruling classes.

At the same time, it is no service to Connolly or the labour movement to falsely eulogise him without being prepared to criticise and learn from his mistakes. The most important lesson from this period points to the need for a revolutionary party. A year and a half after Connolly's execution, the Bolsheviks led the working class to power in Russia, beginning a wave of upheavals that would bring an end to the war. It was an historic tragedy that Connolly was not alive to witness this and to apply its lessons to Ireland. For more analysis on Connolly, we include in the appendix of this edition Peter Hadden's excellent article The real ideas of James Connolly and we would also recommend *Ireland's Lost Revolution*, a publication by the Socialist Party to mark the centenary of the Rising.

Written to prepare socialists for the 1980s

Divide and Rule was written one year after Margaret Thatcher came to power, which itself followed the massive wave of industrial action in Britain known as the "winter of discontent." In the South of Ireland, a significant mass protest of workers swept the country in 1979. In Northern Ireland, it was a time of recovery for the workers' movement. In 1980, the Irish Congress of Trade Unions called a day of action against the Tories' cuts which developed into a half-day regional general strike, the first such strike since the election of Thatcher. Over 50,000 workers marched across the North, including 10,000 in Belfast and 10,000 in Derry.

None of this meant that the Troubles, sectarian division and the complicated issues that flow from them went away, but it did point to the working class as the force capable of overcoming sectarianism and the need for a programme based on class struggle and a socialist alternative. That was evident when the book was written - 1980 saw the first hunger strike against the policy of criminalisation. In 1976, the British government had removed special status for political prisoners. The policy was summed up in Thatcher's famous comment, "Crime is crime is crime." The hunger strike was the escalation of a campaign of protest after republican prisoners first refused to wear prison uniform (the blanket protest) and later refused to slop out (the dirty protest). In 1980, the hunger strike came to an end when it appeared the government was granting concessions, only for a second hunger strike to begin the following year, in which Bobby Sands and nine other republican prisoners would die.

How did Peter Hadden and the Militant - forerunner of the Socialist Party - respond to these issues at the time? Firstly, they were steadfast in their opposition to the "sophisticated apparatus of repression" of the British state, while at the same time pointing out that the methods of groups like the IRA were a "blind alley which eventually serves to strengthen the hand of the state against those at which it is directed."

Crucially, however, they pointed towards united struggle of the working class as the alternative, arguing that the issues at stake should be taken up "in a non-sectarian way by the Labour Movement." They "fought against the sectarian manner in which the issues were posed" and instead "fought for a class approach, with the Labour Movement taking up the issue in class terms", arguing that "in Northern Ireland this means united and joint action by Protestant and Catholic workers, for which there can be no substitute. The entire history of the Labour Movement in Ireland and internationally is proof of the crucial role the Labour Movement has. In 1920, when prisoners in Mountjoy Jail began a hunger strike, a General Strike called by the official Labour and Trade Union Movement in support brought success. The power of rallies and marches based on one side of the community is one thing but strike action at the point of production is an entirely different matter."

This meant taking an independent class position and not simply tailending sectarian or nationalist forces. Instead, the Militant advocated a "programme of prison reform to cover all prisoners which would have included the right to wear their own clothes, to negotiate choice of work and training and education, access to the media, unrestricted numbers of letters and trade union rates of pay." They also argued that the labour movement should review "cases of all those convicted on charges arising out of the Northern Ireland troubles, in order to determine who is, in the eyes of the labour movement, a political prisoner". [5] They recognised there was a difference between those who "joined organisations like the Provos in the mistaken

[5] Peter Hadden, H-Block and Armagh: Issues for the labour movement, Militant Irish Monthly (June 1980) https://www.marxists.org/history/etol/writers/hadden/1980/06/hb-armagh.htm

belief that they were fighting against the present economic system" and those who "were responsible for sectarian atrocities" and were "clearly not political prisoners in any sense in which the labour movement internationally uses the term." Importantly, while this period saw serious sectarian polarisation, it did not stop important industrial action by workers including significant industrial action in health in 1982.

What has any of that got to do with a book dealing with the period leading up to partition? For Peter Hadden, *Divide and Rule* was not some academic exercise but about politically arming a new generation of socialist activists with Marxist ideas. Peter Hadden would later point out, "The answers to the questions how and why partition came about shape both our attitude to the national question today and the programme we put forward to deal with it." [6] The same year, he also wrote a pamphlet on how the labour movement could fight Tory cuts, the title of which summarises this idea - *Common Misery, Common Struggle*.

Relevance for today

Likewise, the republication of *Divide and Rule* is not simply for historical interest. Its purpose is to help a new generation of socialist activists to grapple with the national question. For the Socialist Party, our understanding of the reasons for partition and our analysis that the working class could have avoided it also informs our view of how sectarianism can be challenged today.

That is also true of others, including those who take a different view of the national question. For example, Kevin Meagher, in his short book *A United Ireland: Why unification is invevitable and how it will come about*, states that partition was a "back footed political compromise in order to split the difference between Republicans vying for national self-determination and Loyalists set on having their identity and local hegemony rewarded."[7] Such a simplistic view, devoid of any analysis of the class forces involved in partition, leads logically to the simplistic conclusion that, based on the demographic trends of today, capitalist reunification is not only possible but inevitable. Similarly, some Unionist historians and others would argue that partition was simply the natural outworking of two nations in Ireland and that remains the case today.

The period *Divide and Rule* deals with and the period in which it was written have something in common with today, in that we are seeing increasing militancy of the working class. Prior to the Covid-19 crisis, we saw important struggles, including the historic Harland & Wolff shipyard occupation and the largest industrial action of health workers in Northern Ireland in decades. During the Covid-19 crisis too, workers have shown their preparedness to take collective industrial action to defend their health and

---

6. *Peter Hadden, Troubled Times, Herald Books, 1995*
7. *Kevin Meagher, A United Ireland: Why unification is invevitable and how it will come about*

safety, including the inspiring example of 1,000 workers at the Moy Park site in Portadown walking out in protest against unsafe working conditions. These struggles can be important precursors to even greater battles in the years ahead, which will bring workers - Catholic, Protestant and neither - together.

But it is also likely to be a period of turmoil around the national question, with the dangers of an increase in sectarianism. A key underlying reason is the demographic shift. The 2011 census reflected a watershed moment in Northern Ireland. In 2011, 45% of Northern Ireland's population identified as Catholic and 48% as Protestant. For the first time since partition, the proportion of the population declaring themselves as Protestant, or having been brought up as Protestant, fell below 50%, even after a statistical adjustment for those who initially stated they had no religion. Analysis of the age structure of the 2011 census suggests that the trend away from a Protestant majority is likely to continue. All of this has led to speculation that the next census in 2021 could see the "ironic situation on the centenary of the state where we actually have a state that has a Catholic majority", as Dr Paul Nolan, who specialises in monitoring the peace process and social trends, put it.[8]

This demographic shift is having very obvious political effects. The 2017 Assembly election saw the Unionist political parties returned without a majority at Stormont for the first time in the history of the state. The 2019 general election saw more nationalist than Unionist MPs elected. The impact this will have on the psychology and consciousness of both Protestant and Catholic communities cannot be overstated. The idea that the Union between Britain and the North is secure for the foreseeable future is now gone and increasingly the sense exists that a united Ireland is an inevitability.

Added to this is the impact of Brexit, which has again brought the border centre stage, posing the question of hardened borders either North-South or East-West, ie between Britain and Northern Ireland. The new arrangement would mean that Northern Ireland will, alongside Britain, leave the EU customs union but will remain closely aligned to single market regulations, with customs checks on goods travelling between Britain and Northern Ireland, and potentially regulatory checks as Britain diverges from EU standards. This would effectively mean an East-West border.

This only adds to the legitimate feeling of insecurity about the future of many ordinary Protestants. If there is a perception that their identity and the integrity of the Union is being further diminished and that Northern Ireland is being forced into an "economic united Ireland", it could provoke a serious

---

8. *'Catholic majority possible' in NI by 2021* https://www.bbc.co.uk/news/uk-northern-ireland-43823506

reaction, as we have seen in the past, such as in response to the Anglo-Irish Agreement, which brought thousands onto the streets in 1985, when the second edition of this book was produced.

Added to this is the effect Brexit, alongside years of Tory austerity, has had in increasing support for Scottish independence, which poses sharply the question of the break-up of the United Kingdom. At the same time, Sinn Féin's rise in the South - winning more votes than any other party in the general election in March 2020 - adds to the sense of momentum towards a united Ireland.

All this means that it will not be a return to business as usual for the restored Stormont Executive, with ministers presenting a united front until there is an eruption of a crisis. This can be seen in the response to Covid-19 crisis, where open division has reflected itself on various issues. It is likely we will see more conflict on issues such flags, parades, bonfires and language rights, but also in relation to the competing narratives of history. This can be particularly sharp when it comes to events during the Troubles, as seen with the opposition to the prosecution of Soldier F for his role on Bloody Sunday, but it can also be reflected in terms of events around the centenary of partition.

Centenary of partition

The New Decade, New Approach document, which laid the basis for the restoration of the devolved institutions, talks about a programme of events to mark this centenary. Arlene Foster has even talked about the need to mark it in a way that does "not allow it to divide us, but actually to unite us." However, there is no escaping the reality that Unionists will want to mark it in "in a celebratory way," with suggestions of inviting the Queen to Stormont, while "there are others who will take a different view", as Foster acknowledges. Neither a Unionist nor a nationalist interpretation of partition provides any basis for unity. Only a class analysis of the period can point the way to bringing ordinary people together.

To dispel any idea that this centenary will not be controversial, one only needs to look across the border at the fiasco of the recent attempt by the Southern government to commemorate the Royal Irish Constabulary (RIC), including the notorious Black and Tans. Peter Hadden aptly describes the Black and Tans as embodying "the true spirit of Cromwell, they set about their task, and the toll of their atrocities, the sack of Cork, indiscriminate murder in the Croke Park, etc., is well documented." In fact, not only is it well documented, the atrocities of the Black and Tans are deeply embedded into the psyche of people in the South and Northern Catholics.

As the Socialist Party explained in an article dealing with this controversy, this commemoration was "part of a broader project, championed by Fine Gael especially, to rewrite history. They have been trying for some time to rehabilitate an especially bourgeois, sectarian and pro-imperialist strand of Irish nationalism, symbolised by John Redmond who convinced tens of thousands to die for Empire in the futile slaughter of World War One. Like the RIC, Redmond and his Irish Parliamentary Party were thrown into the ash-heap of history during the revolutionary period."[9]

This is particularly important given that the next few years will see the centenaries of many controversial or divisive aspects of Irish history. This, of course, includes the partition of Ireland, but also the Irish Civil War which saw atrocities committed particularly by the forefathers of Fine Gael. This included massive repression and summary execution, often retaliatory, the most infamous being in Ballyseedy, Co. Kerry, where nine anti-Treaty prisoners were tied to a landmine which was detonated, killing eight with one surviving to tell the tale.

Socialists have a responsibility to bring out the real history of Ireland, North and South, particularly the history of workers uniting and the revolutionary potential that existed in this and other periods. This is why the Socialist Party has produced several publications about this important period, including Ireland's *Lost Revolution* (2016), *Workers' Power in Belfast* (2019) and *Limerick Soviet 1919: The revolt of the bottom dog* (2019).

In 2017, we published for the first time *Common History, Common Struggle*, an important book which Peter Hadden was working on at the time of his untimely death in 2010 which, in many ways, is the sequel to *Divide and Rule*, covering the period after partition up until the late 1960s and the outbreak of the conflict which would become known as the Troubles, with the focus on the revolutionary possibilities at this point. As in the aftermath of partition, "it was the sectarian forces which came out on top after 1969 and it's their version of events which predominates today. There was nothing inevitable about the rise of sectarianism after 1968. Quite the reverse."[10]

The period leading up to partition and the events of the 1960s are very clear examples of an important point made in this book which is worth quoting in full here:

"In the hands of those who could press to the forefront the social issues of the day, the national struggle in Ireland was always capable of drawing the broadest support across the religious barrier between the poor. As in 1798, the attempts by the rulers to wield the club of religious bigotry could be faced and answered.

[9.] *Fine Gael forced to back down from celebrating repressive colonial police,* Manus Lenihan, 2020 https://socialistparty.ie/2020/01/fine-gael-forced-back-celebrating-repressive-colonial-police/
[10.] Peter Hadden, *Common History, Common Struggle,* Herald Books 2017

But the opposite too! On every occasion when the pressure of the upper circles of Irish society has succeeded in jettisoning the social issues from the platforms of those advocating national freedom, the struggle has been stamped with a sectional and ultimately a sectarian character. The way has been paved for the British ruling class to successfully intrude the weapon of sectarianism"

Is a border poll the solution?

The demographic shift, the growing sense of momentum towards a united Ireland and the centenary of partition itself will pose the question for many Catholics of how they can actually achieve Irish unity. Sinn Féin have once again laid out their stall, advocating a "unity referendum" in the next five years. The advocates of a border poll rely on the mathematics of sectarian division and the logic of capitalist economics.

They argue that a united Ireland would be a more efficient capitalist entity than the current set-up. In fact, under the status quo of capitalism, a border poll would be a vote on how to share out misery. As Peter Hadden put it in *Divide and Rule*, "Unity of the capitalist North with the capitalist South is unity of the slums of Belfast with those of Dublin. It would not be the stepping stone to a shining new prosperity that Sinn Féin promise."

As already mentioned, the mood in Protestant working-class areas is already sombre, and there is real fear for the future. As the demographic balance continues to tip away from the Protestant community, they will not simply shrug their shoulders and accept a capitalist united Ireland. In Divide and Rule, Peter Hadden makes the point that for "Protestants of the North, the idea of a capitalist united Ireland is repellent. Their fear of being submerged in a poverty-stricken Republic, in which they would become the discriminated against minority, remains today as it did during the days of Carson. They would resist such a proposal and resist it with force if necessary."

Obviously, a lot has changed in the last 40 years but the thrust of this argument remains true today. Thirty years of sectarian conflict in the form of the Troubles have only served to reinforce these fears. In fact, it is the opposition of the Protestatant population, rather than that of the British state, which is the real barrier to a united Ireland.

At the same time, most Catholics have never been accepting of partition and being imprisoned in a state which treated the Catholic population as second-class citizens for half a century. What was once for many a distant aspiration for a united Ireland now seems like a medium or even short-term prospect. There is no solution in holding out for the day when the

Catholic working class reconcile themselves to the existence of Northern Ireland, given their experience of decades of poverty and repression which, while less acute today, remains for some sections a present reality.

In our view, a border poll is not an instrument to resolve the national question, but in reality would be a dangerous sectarian headcount, the result of which would be contested by the minority. Each community has national aspirations which cannot be ignored or wished away. Catholics have the right to say no to the continuation of the status quo of the Northern state, but Protestants likewise have the right not to be coerced into a united Ireland. Any form of coercion, that is forcing either community into an arrangement against its will, is impermissible. This includes coercion with a democratic facade - ie, a vote which sees one community out vote the other. This would only represent a continuation and escalation of how sectarian forces have operated during the 'peace process.'

No capitalist solution

Twenty-two years on from the Good Friday Agreement, sectarian division has not been overcome. The relative 'peace' is maintained by dozens of permanent 'peace-lines', thousands of armed police and the local enforcement activities of paramilitary groups interested primarily in control of 'their' areas. When all this is insufficient, then temporary peace-lines are thrown up and hundreds of extra police are drafted in.

The ceasefire generation got a taste of the past in the tragic killing of Lyra McKee, a journalist and trade union member who was shot dead by a 'dissident' republican gunman during a riot in Derry. In many ways, all that has been achieved is an 'acceptable level of violence', to borrow a phrase from 1970s Home Secretary Reginald Maudling. Similarly, for many working-class communities, there has been no 'peace dividend' since the end of the conflict.

We have more 'peace walls' than at the end of the Troubles, and two decades after the Good Friday Agreement promised to facilitate integrated education, over 90% of all school students are still educated in segregated schools. But that is not because ordinary people want it that way. Opinion polls consistently show overwhelming support for integrated education. A similar desire is reflected in the 2018 Life and Times survey, in which 76% said they would prefer to live in a mixed neighbourhood and 91% would prefer to work in a mixed workplace.

The political life of Northern Ireland is riddled with division and crises. The most recent three-year impasse at Stormont exposed once again the fragile nature of the 'peace process'. This process has failed to resolve any of the key issues facing working-class people in Northern Ireland. When we do have 'agreements', such as the recent New Decade, New Approach, they are largely agreements to disagree, to kick the can down the road in terms of the fundamental problems of sectarian division, related to culture, identity and the past. The parties in the Assembly are only capable of agreeing on massive attacks on working-class people: the destruction of jobs and services, and tax cuts for the rich, of course. In this sense at least, all the main parties are cut from the same cloth.

After all, the 'solution' of the Good Friday Agreement is rooted in 'elite accommodation based on a consociational model'. By 'elites', the model means literally a handful of people, or even single individuals, 'representing' communities. The elite reach an accommodation – that is, they agree to carve up power and resources – and the communities they supposedly represent live separately. The model presupposes no coming together of people on the ground and holds out no possibility of such a coming together in the future.

For some decades, this was the model implemented in Lebanon. After Lebanon achieved independence from France in 1943, there was an agreement between the largest Christian and Muslim groups which set a fixed ratio of seats in the parliament and guaranteed that the President would be a Christian and the Prime Minister a Sunni Muslim. It was later agreed that the post of Speaker of the Parliament would go to a Shia Muslim. Demographic changes – particularly the numerical growth of the Shia, the most oppressed of the main religious groups – eventually eroded the basis of this accord. In 1975, it all fell to pieces in the civil war that lasted for 15 years.

Workers' movement still key

Just as Lebanon points to the failure of such capitalist attempts to resolve the national question, so too does it offer a glimpse at the type of movement needed to challenge sectarianism. 2019 saw a mass movement shake the country in opposition to corruption, mass unemployment and sectarianism, including in an impressive display of unity, with protesters forming a giant human chain along a 105-mile highway, running from Tyre in the south to Tripoli in the north. The action was designed to show how the mass revolt has united people across religious and regional divides. In the aftermath of the resignation of the Prime Minister, the main slogan from the protests was "all of them means all of them."

In Northern Ireland, the trade unions remain unique as workers' organisations which unite almost 250,000 workers from Protestant, Catholic and other backgrounds, with membership currently increasing, bucking the trend of recent years. Workplaces are often also the main place in which Catholics and Protestants mix. As in the past, trade unionists have been to the fore in response to paramilitary violence, as was the case after the killing of Lyra McKee.

None of this suits the narrative of any of the sectarian forces, who wish to ignore the role of independent and united working-class action. At key points in the history of the North, the trade union movement was able to mobilise ordinary workers in united action – such as demonstrations, walk-outs and strikes – including in response to sectarian threats or attacks and to isolate sectarian forces.

Take the history of one workplace in Northern Ireland as an example, the Harland & Wolff shipyard - a history often tainted with sectarianism, including the infamous 1920 expulsions of Catholic and socialist workers, including so-called "rotten Prods." As Divide and Rule outlines, the previous year saw the famous 1919 engineering strike that originated in the shipyards and united workers across the sectarian divide.

Fifty years later, at the start of the Troubles, trade unionists at Harland & Wolff called a mass meeting of the workforce because Catholic workers had not come to work for fear of sectarian attack. At the meeting, senior shop steward Sandy Scott appealed: "If we act as workers, irrespective of our religion, we can hope for an expansion in work opportunities and a better life". A resolution in opposition to sectarian violence was unanimously passed. The shop stewards then visited the homes of Catholic shipyard workers, successfully appealing to them to return.

Later, when Maurice O'Kane, a Catholic welder, was murdered by the UVF in Harland and Wolff in 1994, shop stewards immediately called thousands of workers out and left the shipyard empty. The shop stewards themselves faced serious threats for this but didn't buckle. Instead, they followed up this action by turning out en-masse to the funeral in an effort to stare down the killers. Finally, in 2019, a united struggle of Protestant, Catholic and other workers saved this historic workplace from closure.

We don't have space here to reference the countless other examples of how ordinary trade unionists tried to stop a slide into sectarian conflict and stood up to sectarian paramilitaries, cutting across tit-for-tat killings. For more on that, people can do no better than to read Common History, Common Struggle. While it isn't possible for sectarian forces to find a lasting solution, it is possible and essential for there to be agreement between working-class people and communities. The working class are capable of coming together in solidarity, entering the stage of history in a decisive fashion as a united force, and finding their way towards socialist ideas.

A major assistance to that process would be the development of a mass working-class political party in the North, and for similar parties to be built in the South and in Britain. These parties will not come into being simply by proclaiming them, but will require events and a new generation moving into struggle. While the situation in the North remains complicated, and there are real dangers inherent in the situation, socialists and those looking for an alternative should be confident that this is possible.

The role of young people

A new generation of young people born since the ceasefires of 1994 are crying out for an alternative. In recent years, they have found themselves in conflict with the social backwardness imposed by the Northern Ireland sectarian parties, especially regarding LGBTQ and abortion rights, and have now won victories when it comes to marriage equality and the right to choose.

An even younger generation has taken part in the international school student strikes in response to the climate crisis. Many were inspired by the movements in support of Corbyn in Britain and Sanders in the US. Socialists should seek to bring out the positive lesson that an alternative can be built, while at the same time pointing to the dangers of a limited approach which seeks to compromise with those hostile to real working-class representation, such as the Blairites in the British Labour Party.

Young people are also frustrated by seemingly forever being imprisoned by Northern Ireland's past and are rightly impatient for a society where all have the right to live in peace, free from intimidation, division and bigotry. Importantly, recent research from Peter Shirlow indicates that 45% of young Protestants do not identify as Unionists, while 55% of young Catholics do not identify as nationalists.[11]

A major point of Divide and Rule is that Ireland, North and South, is not immune from international trends. In the 1920s, the mass revolutionary struggles here were linked to revolutionary movements in Britain, Europe and indeed across the world. These movements not only challenged capitalism but united workers and oppressed people across the lines drawn by capitalism and imperialism in their efforts to divide and rule. The same was true in the 1960s, when young people in particular drew inspiration from the civil rights movement in the US and revolutionary struggles across the world.

Today, we live in a more globalised society than ever, and many young people have an even more developed internationalist outlook. Struggles across the world inspire each other, as was seen with the mass movements which swept the globe in 2019, from Chile to Lebanon and Hong Kong.

---

[11]. *NI survey suggests 50% neither unionist nor nationalist*
https://www.bbc.co.uk/news/uk-northern-ireland-48702235

As already mentioned, the central lesson of Divide and Rule is the need to build a working-class alternative, armed with socialist politics and capable of tying together workers in common struggle. If that does not come about, sectarianism will reassert itself, as was seen with the expulsions from the shipyards shortly after the 1919 engineering strike. Similarly, 1932 saw an inspiring and united struggle of unemployed workers in Belfast during the outdoor relief strike, but the failure to build a political force capable of harnessing and channelling this solidarity meant that sectarian pogroms were again the order of the day by 1935. If a socialist alternative is not built, it will not mean an indefinite continuation of an imperfect peace, but a retrenchment back into sectarian conflict.

A new working-class party would be forced to deal with all the complicated questions which sectarian division throws up from its beginning. It could not simply unite people around the 'bread and butter' issues and put off discussion on the contentious issues until a later date. Instead, it would have to adopt an independent class position on a range of issues from the outset.

For socialism in Ireland

Most importantly, it would have to strive to raise the sights of working-class people beyond the real problems of poverty and division today, and towards the possibilities inherent in a socialist future. As Peter Hadden summed it up in *Troubled Times*, "Socialism means taking the major industry and all key services into public ownership and running them democratically, with need replacing profit as the motive. It means no privileged elite, only the right of people themselves to manage their own affairs. It means creating an international brotherhood and sisterhood, a unity based on respect of difference and in which all national and minority rights would be guaranteed. It is the unity of the working class, built in the struggle for such a society that will solve the national problem in Ireland."

A new mass party must base itself upon the fundamental unity of the working class in the unions, workplaces and in struggles. The maximum unity of working-class people in this island would be the breaking down of all forces that divide us, including the border. The Socialist Party therefore advocates a socialist Ireland, with full and equal rights for all communities, including the protection of minorities.

However, one cannot be opposed to coercion under capitalism but view it as permissible under socialism, which by its very nature is a higher form of democracy, with working-class people in control of every aspect of their lives, instead of the diktats of the markets and CEOs. Protestant working-class people have legitimate fears about a 'united ireland'. Common struggle can alleviate those fears, but they are deep-rooted.

While not advocating it, socialists should accept the right of predominantly Protestant communities in the North to opt out of a unitary socialist state, with the right to autonomy or even separation. That would not, however, mean the maintenance of the current border, which most Catholics would oppose, but an alternative arrangement, which may be cumbersome, but would be possible to peacefully and democratically agree in a spirit of solidarity, compromise and mutual respect.

Socialism cannot be confined to one country and would require an international struggle to transform society. The Socialist Party is in favour of a socialist Ireland in an equal and voluntary socialist federation with Scotland, England and Wales, which in turn would be part of a wider European socialist federation or confederation. That too would have to be a completely voluntary and equal arrangement, and not based on any form of coercion, as Karl Marx argued when he first raised a similar idea. Writing to his collaborator Engels on the issue of independence for Ireland, he said "after the separation may come federation." [12]

Such an idea has been derided by those from a republican tradition but, not only would such an arrangement be of practical importance, it is the natural outworking of international working-class solidarity and co-operation, something starkly missing from the capitalist classes' response to the Covid-19 crisis. Such a demand is also a way of winning the ear of Protestant workers who, unfortunately, associate socialism with narrow Irish nationalism, because of the empty rhetoric of republican groups but also the record of those on the left who have backed them.

We live in a turbulent world. The Covid-19 crisis will be a defining historic moment. Workers will have to organise, fight back and thus learn lessons about the reality of capitalism and the need for socialist change. They will be assisted in that process by looking at the rich history of the socialist and workers' movement. We are in no doubt that the republication of this book can make an important contribution.

The struggle for solutions to the issues which divide workers, including the national question, is not easy. It's not for nothing that one of the leaders of the Russian revolution, Leon Trotsky, described the national question as "most labyrinthine and complex". Nonetheless, the Socialist Party has confidence in the power, capacity and ingenuity of the working class, which has been demonstrated amidst this crisis. If you agree and find this book useful, we encourage you to discuss with us further and join us in the vital struggle for socialist change.

[12.] *Letter from Marx to Engels, 2nd November , 1867*
https://www.marxists.org/archive/marx/works/1867/letters/67_11_02-abs.htm

INTRODUCTION

By Peter Hadden
1986 Edition

The partition of Ireland was a conscious act on the part of British imperialism chiefly intended to divide the working class along sectarian lines. As the recent troubles have made the publication of works on Irish history more profitable, a host of academics have presented ever newer accounts of the division of the country. In the midst of this welter of publication the above straightforward fact about partition has often been lost sight of. In particular this has been the case among those who have spent their energies seeking some justification to rationalize and excuse the division of Ireland, so that they, in turn, may excuse themselves from opposing this division. Above all, this is true of those who justify partition with the completely false idea that the division of the country somehow reflects the existence of two separate nations in Ireland.

The history of partition itself and, indeed, the entire past history of Ireland completely refute such ideas. Partition was a desperate act, carried out in defence of class interests. Over the previous centuries no less desperate measures were effected by the ruling class in Britain, all likewise designed to further their economic objectives.

Since the first Norman invasion the entire history of Ireland has been a history of struggle against subjugation, conquest and exploitation. This struggle has at all times been more than a battle for mere independence. Conquest meant more than the overrunning of a country. It meant the overthrow of a social system. At every stage the fight to obtain "freedom" has been driven on by the desire of sections of the Irish people to remove one or other form of class rule and oppression. The motor of Irish history has been the social exploitation of its people.

The early clan system, a form of primitive communism [1], was the first

---

[1.] *Primitive communism is a way of describing hunter-gatherer societies, where resources are shared with all members of a group, in accordance with individual needs. Pre-Norman Ireland had a social order with remnants of primitive communism. Kings were elected and subject to removal; the territory and cattle were the common property of the clan. Sharing was an obligation, subject to means. On the other hand, "unfree" classes – slavery – existed. The laws and customs were hierarchical and sexist, though much less so than those of feudalism.*

casualty of the Norman Conquest. Imposed was an alien social system based on private ownership of wealth, with rights of inheritance and property sacrosanct.

Landlordism was imposed by the sword. The native Irish were driven from whole tracts of their land, which were given to the "planters" brought across from England and Scotland. These people were intended to be the rock on which British rule would be based and the seemingly endless revolts of the Irish would perish. Sadly for these rulers, one generation after another of these planters became rooted in Ireland, modified and assimilated the customs of their neighbours – in short became Irish.

Rebellion stirred not only among the original inhabitants of the country but among these settlers also. To differing degrees, both were bound by the system of foreign exploitation. To rule in the face of these revolts the British chose to divide. Religion was the chosen instrument of division. Religious intolerance, the fostering of mutual suspicion, hatred and violence between Catholic and Protestant – this became the shield of the ruling administration against the overthrow by the people.

With these methods an entire social system was dissolved. With precisely the same methods Irish society was prevented from undergoing social development in line with other countries. Landlordism meant more than the imposition of terrible conditions on the mass of the Irish peasantry. It meant that the surplus wealth produced by those who toiled on the land was sent to England and consumed by a parasitic breed of absentee owners. The result was the stifling of any nascent industrial development.

Once again foreign domination was clearly shown to be domination by the foremost class interest in the ruling nation. The industrial revolution in Britain in the eighteenth and nineteenth centuries brought the accelerated development of new industry and technique. Previously unheard-of wealth fell into the hands of the rising capitalist class.

No competition would this class sanction from Ireland and Irish industry. Because of foreign domination and the restrictions imposed by the landlord system, Irish industry was inevitably much weaker than its rival. As British capitalism was slipping out of the womb, Irish capitalism had not passed the foetus stage. It was a tiny organism, dwarfed by semi-feudal social relationships.

Through trade restrictions, tariff barriers, etc., the British capitalists determined that the Irish foetus would be aborted. Ireland was to remain an agricultural colony, a feeding machine for the growing and hungry cities of industrial England. Her offspring, driven by misery and starvation from the land, were to be sucked to the English cities, where they would provide additional cheap labour for the new bosses.

Against such domination the various class interests in Ireland struggled. They did so, however, in differing ways and with vastly differing degrees of determination. Towards the close of the eighteenth century conditions ripened for revolt. The peasantry, the artisans, the embryo of the proletariat, the shopkeepers and small businessmen, even sections of the "Irish" aristocracy, were seething with the spirit of rebellion.

In 1798 the United Irishmen, an armed and secret movement built up over previous years, rose in rebellion. It was one of the greatest movements of the Irish against domination. It welded the Protestant petty bourgeoisie of Belfast and the Protestant tenants of Antrim and Down together with the Catholic peasantry of Connaught, Wexford and elsewhere. But as one of the greatest events in the history of Ireland it revealed in the starkest form the bitter lessons of that history.[2]

From the outset the rising was marked by treachery and confusion. Different areas rose at different times in uncoordinated revolt. Spies and traitors assured that the plans were known to the garrison before the event. Arrests and seizures of arms weakened the muscle of the rising before it even started.

Such chaos was not accidental. It reflected the attitudes of the various class interests involved. The sporadic nature of the fighting demonstrated the absence of a developed bourgeois class neither anxious nor willing to fight for independence. Only in the North was the rising bourgeoisie, because of the greater development of manufacture, able to play a role of any significance. In the rest of the country the aristocrats largely backed the establishment and the small embryonic capitalist class was too weak and too timid to take up the leadership of the struggle. The fighting outside the north east was almost entirely conducted by the peasantry.

Even those from among the more "well-to-do" who did support the aims of the United Irishmen looked to distinctly different methods of struggle than did their "comrades" among the peasantry and the lower orders in the towns. More fearful of the popular movement and of the "communistic" ambitions they attributed to some within it, they counselled against a go-it-alone policy on the part of the Irish.

Instead they looked to the French to come and "liberate" their country for them. United Irish leaders like Henry Joy McCracken and Jemmy Hope

---

[2.] *Petty bourgeoisie or petit-bourgeoisie is the name used by Marxists to refer to sections of the middle class who are small-scale capitalists, ie small business owners* were quick to see such "foreign-aid men" for what they were. Hope, in his memoirs written forty years after the rising, commented:

> "The appearance of the French fleet in Bantry Bay brought the rich farmers and shopkeepers into the societies, and with them all the corruption essential to the objects of the British Ministry, to foster rebellion, to possess the power of subduing it and to carry a legislative Union. The new adherents alleged, as a reason for their former reserve, that they thought the societies only a combination of the poor to get the property of the rich."

Nation states arose from the development of capitalism. To the rising capitalist class in countries like England and France fell the lot of sweeping aside feudal particularism, knitting together their national territory and attaining recognition as a separate nation. To replace the power of the feudal heads of society with those of the capitalist state, the bourgeois drew behind them all the oppressed social orders. Having used the lower layers of society as a club to lay waste the vestiges of feudal power and consolidate their own class rule, the bourgeoisie set about curtailing the activities and demands of these layers, very often re-imposing the superstructure of the old system in order to do so.

The Irish bourgeoisie came on to the scene of history late. They emerged to find their weak arms pinned to their sides by the power of their rulers and rivals in England. 1798 proved that they had neither the strength nor the inclination to lead any struggle for independence. The historical mission of the bourgeoisie – to take the leadership of the downtrodden sections of society and carve a place in the world for a nation of their own based on capitalist social relations – they were unable to fulfil. It was not these men of property but those described by the United Irishmen leader Wolfe Tone as the "men of no property" who provided the only consistent and reliable members of the United Irishmen societies and who had been and would remain the only consistent revolutionary force in Irish history. The Irish bourgeoisie, the middle classes and the Irish "establishment" followed the defeat of 1798 by more and more willingly bowing the knee to their masters more and more openly assisting the repression of the social movements of the Irish masses in the cities and on the land.

The 1798 defeat was followed in 1801 by the passing of an Act of Union bridging Ireland directly under the rule of Westminster. Thereafter the struggle for independence was sharply divided in form according to class interest. By independence the propertied classes meant simply repeal of the Union so that economic exploitation would continue, but with an Irish face. At no stage were these interests prepared to lead a struggle even for such independence. To have done so would have entailed mobilizing the propertyless class, the peasantry and the seeds of the proletariat, and the well-to-do were motivated more by fear of these classes than by the irritation they suffered through foreign domination. Whenever the middle classes elbowed themselves into positions of leadership in any movement purporting to oppose the foreign rule of their country, it was only to separate the "national" demands for independence from the social conditions and social objectives from which they took root. Ultimately their role was to betray that movement.

For the peasants and, as they developed, the working class, independence meant more than the lifting of the chains of foreign rule. It was seen as the breaking of the bonds of social exploitation. From the lower levels of society, because of their oppression, came the only truly dynamic and revolutionary force to fight for national independence. During the nineteenth century the issue of the land provided the focal point of Irish struggle. But by their very nature the movements of these peasants tended to be sporadic and difficult to organise. Peasants exist on small plots of land. Physically they live apart from their fellow beings. Their mode of existence leans them towards individual terror rather than collective action. Without some external reservoir of support and leadership, movements of the peasantry have a tendency to be spontaneous outbursts of individual activity. By contrast industrial workers stand for eight hours every day beside their fellow workers, endure the same conditions in the factories, earn broadly the same wage, live in similar circumstances. Their very condition of existence presses them towards collective and united action. Common misery teaches the virtue of solidarity.

While workers can rely on their own class for strength, peasants seek the leadership of other classes. The country always follows the town. For the Irish masses on the land the real task as the nineteenth century opened was to find a social group among the urban population from whom they could obtain leadership. There was no shortage of middle-class politicians who were quite prepared to accelerate their political careers by involving themselves to a degree in popular agitation. Into such a category would fall "leaders" of this period like "the Liberator" Daniel O'Connell. In the mysterious legends which sometimes pass as the official versions of Irish history, O'Connell lives on as the champion of the people who led them to

Catholic emancipation and to within a breath of independence. Researchers do not have to dig too deep to uncover the true attitudes of this man of the establishment to the social aspirations of the Irish people.

O'Connell's contempt for the real revolutionary struggle was demonstrated in 1803. It was in this year that Robert Emmett led a rising with little support except in the solidly working-class districts of Dublin. "The Liberator", caring little for liberty at this time, turned out on sentry duty for Major Sirr, the officer in charge of the crown forces. This was neither the first nor the last time the true colours of O'Connell came out. After his huge success in a by-election in Clare in 1829 he took sides on all key issues of the day at Westminster. In 1832 he opposed the introduction of the poor law for Ireland. In 1836 he voted for a "Regulations of Factory" Bill, which exempted children of 12-13 from the Eight-Hour Day Act of 1833. It is said he sold his vote for £700. [3]

O'Connell did lead the agitation for the repeal of the Act of Union in the 1830s and 1840s. He led it so far and no further. After a series of "monster meetings" he called for an enormous protest at Clontarf in 1843. The meeting was banned and the "bluff" was called. To go ahead meant a physical challenge to the establishment. O'Connell cancelled the meeting and with this one action deflated absolutely his entire campaign. As the United Irishmen leader, Henry Joy McCracken, just before his death in 1798, had commented with the insight of prophecy: "The rich always betray the poor."

At this stage the repeal of the Act of Union could only have been achieved by a revolutionary and physical struggle. The British ruling class would not have granted it peacefully. What caused O'Connell and his like to draw back at a certain point was the impenetrable force field of their own class interests. Consciously or unconsciously the peasantry were striving to abolish landlordism and possess the soil. The middle class and the representatives of the Irish bourgeoisie baulked at the prospect. Even more abjectly they fell into the laps of British capital.

With no possibility of leadership coming from the middle classes, those at the head of the land agitation increasingly leaned towards links with the workers. And the absence of any developed working class in Ireland led them to seek to foster links with the British workers. Through the Young Irelanders and the Fenians to the Land League agitation in the 1870s, the leadership of this revolt became increasingly plebeian in outlook. Karl Marx,

---

[3] *Poor Laws were a system of poor relief that developed out of the codification of late-medieval and Tudor-era laws in 1587–1598. The system continued until the modern welfare state emerged after the Second World War.*

in founding the First International Workingmen's Association, chose to develop links with the Fenians, at the same time criticizing their terroristic
methods.Later Michael Davitt, the leader of the Land League, consciously
sought to ally his involvement with the growing labour movement.[4]

The absence of a developed proletariat in the Irish cities swung the gaze
of these movements to Britain. The last decades of the nineteenth and the
first of this century changed this. In Belfast, Cork, Dublin and elsewhere
the Irish working class began to develop their own organisations, industrial
and then political.

A new class, capable of taking the leadership of the national struggle,
drawing behind it the tenants and all the downtrodden, was formed. Nothing could be the same again. The only real fight for liberation thereafter
was the fight of the workers supported by the poor of the land. James Connolly, a pioneer of the labour movement in terms of both organisation and
of ideas, drew the appropriate conclusion.

Connolly, with his clear understanding that "only the working class remain as the incorruptible inheritors of the fight for freedom in Ireland",
was echoing the theory of permanent revolution put forward by Trotsky.
During the first years of this century Trotsky explained that, in a less developed country, the basic tasks of the bourgeois revolution, because of the in-
ability of the weak native bourgeoisie to carry these through, fall to the
working class. [5]

The workers, by taking power into their own hands, could achieve such
ends as the distribution of the land to the peasants, tasks which the bourgeoisie proved incapable of fulfilling. But the working class would not stop
there. They could also carry out their own historic goals, taking control of
the economy and carrying through the socialist revolution.

Trotsky's theory brilliantly predicted the course of the Russian Revolution of 1917. In the works of Connolly, because he was capable of drawing
identical conclusions to those of Trotsky, there is contained a clear fore-
warning of the consequences of the struggle for independence falling into
the hands of the middle class.

Connolly's entire lifetime of struggle within the labour movement was
largely devoted to an attempt to press this movement to draw the lessons
of Irish history and place itself at the head of the national struggle. In so
doing Connolly was not advocating that the movement forsake its own objectives. Rather, just as Trotsky explained in relation to Russia and elsewhere, Connolly argued that the objectives of the socialist revolution and

4 *The attitude of Marx and Engels to the Fenian movement is dealt with in various books. For more
information, see https://www.marxists.org/history/erol/uk.hightide/cwm-fenian.pdf*
5. *For more information, see James Connolly's Labour in Irish History & Leon Trotsky's Permanent
Revolution and Results and Prospects*

those of national freedom were completely interwound. Only a few weeks before his death in 1916, he boldly stated his objectives:

> "We are out for Ireland and for the Irish. But who are the Irish? Not the rack-renting, slum-owning landlord; not the sweating, profit-grinding capitalist; not the sleek and oily lawyer; not the prostitute pressmen – the hired liars of the enemy. Not these are the Irish upon whom the future depends. Not these, but the Irish working class, the only secure foundation upon which a nation can be reared." (*Workers' Republic, 8, April, 1916.*)

The property-owning classes have been incapable of pursuing the fight against national domination in Ireland. In particular, since the defeat of the 1798 rebellion, this has been an unmistakable fact of Irish history. The involvement of these classes in any aspect of the national struggle has always been with the objective and the effect of dissolving the social basis and amputating the social demands of that struggle.

Invariably the effect of any dilution of the social aspect of the national question has led to a weakening of that struggle and a strengthening of the hand of British imperialism. The tactic of "divide and rule", of setting Catholic against Protestant, has again and again been used in Ireland. But history shows, not once but repeatedly, that the oppressed masses are capable of overcoming religious divisions and withstanding the attempts of the exploiters to set them apart. Unity of the oppressed has always been possible on the basis of opposition to oppression. The United Irishmen drew support from all the downtrodden layers of society, Catholic and Protestant, precisely because these people saw it as a movement for social change. Again during the nineteenth century, the bolder the social appeal of those involved in the land agitation, the more striking the results they achieved in terms of the unity of Catholic and Protestant. Thus the land war of Davitt and the Land League received support from the Catholics of the South as well as from the poorer sections of the Protestant tenants in the North. The development of labour in opposition to the industrial slavery imposed on the workers of Belfast and Dublin represented the highest ever form of unity against social oppression.

In the hands of those who could press to the forefront the social issues of the day, the national struggle in Ireland was always capable of drawing the broadest support across the religious barrier between the poor. As in 1798, the attempts by the rulers to wield the club of religious bigotry could be faced and answered.

But the opposite too! On every occasion when the pressure of the upper circles of Irish society has succeeded in jettisoning the social issues from the platforms of those advocating national freedom, the struggle has been stamped with a sectional and ultimately a sectarian character. The way has been paved for the British ruling class to successfully intrude the weapon of sectarianism.

These were the essential lessons which the Irish labour movement needed to learn as it developed during the first decades of this century. The middle and upper classes had left the national struggle in shreds before deserting to the camp of the enemy. Economic interest always overcame "historic" and "patriotic" sentiment. It was left to the workers to prevent a sham and divisive struggle for notional independence. The task of drawing upon the experience of the past and of uniting the people, North and South, Catholic and Protestant, fell to the working class.

This is the background to the stormy events of the two decades which preceded the division of the country in 1920-21. Through partition, imperialism carried the tactic of "divide and rule" further than ever before. They did so because the situation, particularly in the years 1918-21, posed the greatest dangers they had ever encountered in Ireland. These were years of revolutionary upheaval on an unprecedented scale. Strikes, even general strikes, land seizures, even the establishment of forms of soviets in certain areas, took place. [6] At issue was not only the question of whether Ireland would be self-governing, but the greater question of whether or not the capitalist system would survive. The purpose of partition was to disorient and check the movement of the working class. In this objective, and for reasons explained later, it was successful.

This pamphlet has been produced in order to explain the real reasons for partition. Its conclusion is that this evil could have been averted, but only on the basis of a movement of the working class to change society. Unfortunately the leaders of Irish labour failed to digest the conclusions from Irish history which Connolly had so clearly presented before them. Above all, in the years after 1916, when Connolly was dead, they handed the struggle against national domination to a group of middle-class nationalists. With the words "Labour must wait" these nationalists emulated their predecessors and ditched the driving social motivation of the revolt. The result was a movement for independence which the bosses were capable of restraining within sectarian bounds. Irish labour, the mightiest force in Irish society if only it could be harnessed to a fighting programme and leadership, was relegated to a back seat.

The Irish working class could have averted partition. More than this, only

---

[6.] *Soviet literally means 'council', referring to the democratic bodies estbalished by workers during the 1905 Russian revolution and again in 1917. These saw delegates elected from different workplaces come together and discuss the future and running of the revolution. Similar organs of workers' power have been found in countless other revolutions, including in Ireland, most famously the Limerick Soviet of 1919.*

the Irish working class could have done so. If the demands of labour for a socialist Ireland and for international working-class solidarity had been to the forefront, the efforts of British imperialism to sow division could have been thwarted. This is the fundamental conclusion which stands out from every aspect of the period covered in this pamphlet.

Likewise, if the labour movement alone was capable of preventing partition, only the labour movement can overcome it today. If, at the beginning of the century, when the working class were first attempting to find their feet as a social force, they alone were capable of successfully opposing imperialism, how much more so today when the workers, in terms of numbers and specific social weight, are now the predominant force in Irish society.

Partition created a sectarian statelet in the North, maintained in existence through enormous subventions from Britain and based on the perpetration of sectarian division. In the South there emerged a country with formal independence but in which the domination by British and foreign capital has been maintained. There is today no way forward for either part of the country on the basis of capitalism.

Yet the idea has been projected in some quarters, even some on the "left", that the objectives of their struggle should be to reunify the country on a capitalist basis and only then proceed to the establishment of socialism.

Those who fail to learn from the mistakes of the past are doomed to repeat them. Between 1918 and 1921 the nationalists of Sinn Féin argued that first there must be independence and then, in the context of "freedom", the struggle for socialism could proceed "if necessary"! Today's notion of first "reunification" and then socialism is an even more heinous version of this same policy which had such disastrous consequences sixty years ago.

Those who argue for such a strategy have learned nothing from Irish history, let alone from the history of the working class internationally. They have failed, more than sixty years after his death, to appreciate the most basic of the teachings of Connolly. They have failed to realize the significance of the Marxist theory of "Permanent Revolution" or to see how this was borne out by the action of Lenin, Trotsky and the Bolsheviks in 1917.

To separate class issues from the key aspect of the national question which remains to be solved in Ireland, that is the reunification of the country, has an even worse effect today than in the past. Those who advocate such a thing do not stand in the tradition of Tone, Emmet, Davitt or Connolly. They must take their place in the shadows of Grattan, Flood, the "foreign-aid men" of 1798, O'Connell, Griffith and De Valera.

As in the past, the owners of property have today no interest in the national struggle, that is the question of reunification of the country. Neither of the capitalist parties in the South, Fianna Fail or Fine Gael, has either the stomach or the desire to rule the North. Politicians such as Haughey and Blaney, who occasionally deliver some bombastic sermon on this question, invariably do so solely to divert the attention of the Southern working class from their economic problems.[7]

Equally the right wing Nationalist parties in the North, into which category can now be put the SDLP, have neither any strategy nor any intention of conducting a real fight against partition. Nor does the apparently more "radical" nationalism of Sinn Féin offer any way forward.

The basis of Sinn Féin's position is that partition must be ended before the working class can be united and therefore before the social and class questions can be resolved. When the camouflage of socialist sounding phrases are taken away, Sinn Féin's arguments amount to nothing more than a repetition of De Valera's disastrous message of 1918 – "Labour must wait". In the last analysis, no different from the SDLP and every other shade of nationalism, they advocate the utopian pipe dream of capitalist reunification.

For the working class, reunification poses no attraction on a capitalist basis. Unity of the capitalist North with the capitalist South is unity of the slums of Belfast with those of Dublin and of the dole queues which in the country as a whole contain almost 300,000 workers. Above all, to the Protestants of the North, the idea of a capitalist united Ireland is repellent. Their fear of being submerged in a poverty-stricken Republic, in which they would become the discriminated against minority, remains today as it did during the days of Carson. They would resist such a proposal and resist it with force if necessary.[8]

During the 1960s British imperialists, because of their changed interests, above all their penetration of the Southern economy, raised the possibility of a move towards the reunification of the country. They quickly found that the sectarianism which they had generated in the past refused to self-destruct. Imperialism, despite its desire to have the Irish question resolved in this manner, has been forced to retreat. Today the ending of partition has been pushed to the back of the minds of the ruling class by the realities of the situation. The masters of the capitalist system have been made to realize that capitalist reunification is ruled out.

So too should those other forces who advance this dream. During the War of Independence the methods of guerrilla struggle adopted by the IRA proved incapable of defeating the forces of imperialism. Failing to learn from

---

[7.] *This refers to Charlie Haughey and Neil Blaney. Both were Fianna Fáil ministers who were implicated in the 'arms crisis' scandal, where funds were raised in the South for the Provisional IRA. At the time this book was written, Haughey was the leader of Fianna Fáil and Taoiseach.*
[8.] *Edward Carson was a leader of Unionism in Ireland in the period this book focuses on.*

this, the Provisional IRA and others have conducted a campaign for more than a decade, based on similar methods but in a less favourable situation in every sense. But quite apart from their false methods of struggle the belief of the Provisional leaders that the country can be united other than on the basis of socialism is a utopian illusion.

In reality they, and others who pursue a similar strategy, are playing with the prospect of a sectarian civil war. This would result, not in reunification, but most likely in a repartition of the country through the creation of a wholly Protestant enclave in a reduced area of what is now Northern Ireland. If Connolly could warn the labour movement in 1914 of the disastrous consequences of partition, Marxists today are correct in warning against the horrendous consequences of such a strategy. Not reunification but an Israeli-type situation with an entrenched statelet surrounded by refugee camps and displaced persons who could not be integrated into the shattered economy of the Southern state – this could be the catastrophic result. Despite the setback caused by the Anglo-Irish agreement, this is still the least likely development.

In the North the potential for a mighty class movement drawing together Protestant and Catholic workers has been demonstrated many times over, most particularly during the 1982 Health workers strike and in the campaigns of support which were organised. Such movements challenge the non-party political stand of the right wing trade union leaders. The demand for the creation of a political party, based on the trade unions, which could represent the working class is now taking on flesh.

In the South the working class has shown its determination and its power many times in recent years, in the 1979 Post Office strike, in the massive demonstrations over PAYE, in the occupation of Ranks flour mill, the Clondalkin paper mill and in other struggles. As in the North this industrial might has not been reflected politically.[9]

The reunification of Ireland means first the development of such struggles and linking together in common action of the working class and their organisations, North and South. It means the unity of workers in the North, the unity of Northern workers with their Southern brothers and sisters on the basis of a joint struggle for socialism. As a part of the socialist transformation of society the border can be removed. On the basis of Connolly's writings, and of his actual participation as a Marxist in the labour movement, it can be said without a doubt that this is the conclusion he would have drawn had he lived to experience the implementation of the 1920 Government of Ireland Act, the subse-

---

9. *PAYE stands for 'Pay As You Earn'. If you are an employee, you normally pay tax through PAYE.*

quent treaty with Sinn Féin in the South and the events which followed.

The Irish Labour Party has been held back by the participation of its right wing and careerist leaders in a series of disastrous coalitions with the right wing capitalist party Fine Gael. Labour's rank and file together with the rank and file of the trade unions are moving against coalition. The working class will break the Labour Party free of the shackles of coalitionism, will move Labour towards its independent socialist roots and the Party will then be poised for explosive growth. [10]

The programme of Marxism in Ireland today finds its roots in the ideas of Connolly no less than in the programme and experience of the greatest Marxists of the past, Marx, Engels, Lenin and Trotsky. Connolly opposed the idea of labour entering a coalition with its enemies. Those who insist that labour in the South must fight independently on socialist policies stand in his tradition. Connolly proposed that the Irish trade unions establish a Labour Party. Those who advocate that the trade unions in the North must immediately form such a party stand with him on this question. Connolly fought for the ownership of the economy to be placed in the hands of the working class. He struggled to achieve decent working conditions, decent wages, and shorter hours for all workers. Today the Marxist programme of Militant, for a 35-hour week, for a minimum wage tied to the cost of living, for guaranteed work for all, and for the nationalisation of the banks, finance houses and major monopolies is simply his programme placed in the context of present conditions. Connolly fought to mobilise the working class to remove all aspects of imperialism, military and economic, from Ireland. He also struggled resolutely against sectarianism and urged action on the part of the organisations of the working class to eliminate this evil. By assisting in the formation of the Irish Citizen Army in 1913, and in maintaining thereafter this body in existence as the armed wing of the trade-union movement, he helped construct the first army of the working class in Europe. His ideas are today maintained and developed through the demand for the withdrawal of the British troops from the North and their replacement by a trade union defence force capable of defending all workers against sectarian attack. Above all, and it is the purpose of this pamphlet to underscore this point, Connolly's tradition is maintained by the labour movement adopting a socialist approach to the question of partition, placing in its banner the objective of the unity in struggle of the working class throughout Ireland and the establishment of a socialist united Ireland.

---

[10] *It should be noted that this book was written in the 1980s when the Militant was part of the Labour Party and arguing within it for socialist policies. Since then, there has be significant shift to the right among the former social democratic parties, including in the Irish Labour Party*

Part I

CHAPTER ONE

Land & Capital

Class Conflict & Home Rule Before 1914

"The history of all hitherto existing society i.e. recorded history is the history of class struggle." With these famous words Karl Marx and Friedrich Engels in 1848 introduced their Communist Manifesto. Irish history, especially during the first years of this century, as it has been principally recorded, would appear to refute this remark. Armed Unionist reaction in the form of the Ulster Volunteer Force, thousands of nationalist volunteers, sectarianism and ultimately partition – all would seem to qualify Irish history as an exception. Religion, not class, would seem to be the motor of development. And so it has been treated by most historians.

Mountains of literature have been written of the subject of the division of Ireland. But very little has been said! In most accounts the class struggle has been relegated to a poor second place. But Marx's statement is not only valid – it is key to understanding and interpretation of events during this period and since.

In 1870 the Liberal administration at Westminster introduced a Land Act which mildly reformed the iniquitous system of landlordism in Ireland. Improvements carried out by the tenant to the land were no longer to be accredited to the landlord. If a tenant was evicted for some reason other than non-payment of rent, the landlord could be forced to pay compensation.

This mild rebuke to the landlords did nothing to resolve the land question. It merely aggravated the landlords by imposing the sting of minute restrictions on their activities, while, at the same time, it added to the thirst of the tenants for more substantial reform.

But Prime Minister Gladstone's first Land Act was an indication of a process of transformation taking place at the top of society. In earlier decades the interests of the landlords had been resolutely defended. Revolt after revolt of the tenants and landless masses had been put down in blood.

All the trappings of the system of "British justice" in Ireland, the courts and the judiciary, served and faithfully upheld the interests of landlordism.

For the aristocratic establishment, repression had been the favourite weapon to use against the Irish. Yet the policy of repression and evictions held the movement back with one hand but provided it with nutrition on the other. It solved nothing. So long as the interests of the landlords were held to be supreme, no other policy was possible. By the last decade of the nineteenth century the power of the landowning aristocracy in Britain was firmly in decline. Industrial capital had become the predominant interest in the state.

For the hard-headed business acumen of the Victorian capitalists a better solution needed to be found. Why should they constantly place the stability of their system at risk by provoking dangerous and contagious ideas of revolt in Ireland in order to protect and maintain the bloated gentry? Inexorably as the power and wealth of society moved from the hands of the landlords into the grasp of the industrial bourgeoisie, the pressure to find a settlement to the land question grew.

Most immediately sensitive to this change were the English Liberals. At this time the Liberal Party was the major party of the capitalists in Britain. In order to safeguard the interest of capital they strove to placate the demands of the land-hungry peasants. Their early efforts fell too far short of the mark to prove effective. They merely increased the appetite of the tenant for real reforms. The 1870 Act resulted, not in an ebbing of the land agitation, but in its intensification.

With the repeal of the Corn Laws, the development of the world market and of new techniques of production, prices obtained in the market by the producers of agricultural products fell. The tenants found themselves unable to pay their rents. Those with smallholdings found their enterprises particularly unprofitable. Landlords retaliated by attempting to evict the smallholders and consolidate the land into more economic units – with higher rents, of course. During the late 1870s, as agricultural prices fell, the tenants found that the 1870 Act offered them no security from eviction. The Land League led by Michael Davitt held meetings of more than 10,000 to resist the evictions of their neighbours. To the horror of the British ruling class, these "peasants" were arming themselves for the purpose. [11]

Davitt was answered with the traditional methods of the establishment. He and other leaders of the Land League were arrested. Meetings were banned and suppressed. Davitt was a revolutionary leader whose ideas and methods could not and would not be tolerated by the bosses. His demand was not merely for land reform, but for land nationalisation. Unlike many of his predecessors at

---

[11.] *The Corn Laws were tariffs and other trade restrictions on imported food and grain enforced in the United Kingdom between 1815 and 1846.*

the head of similar revolts, he was conscious of the need to link the struggles of the tenants with those of the workers in the cities. A decade after the Land League agitation, he was attempting to create an Irish Federated Trade and Labour Union. Equally his outlook was not marred by the narrow horizons of nationalism. Looking at the English cities he saw a potential and powerful ally in the mass of the English workers. In later years, while in England, he was deeply involved in the struggle to create the British Labour Party.

Such ideas were dynamite to the bosses. The "excesses" of the land agitation were to be met with the full weight of repression. Precisely because Davitt and those like him were the most "dangerous" type of leaders to emerge from Ireland, an understanding of the need to tackle the root cause of the unrest grew in the minds of the capitalists.

On one side the traditional methods of repression were used. A special Coercion Bill was introduced by the government in order to give itself even more draconian powers. Repression merely accelerated the struggle and hardened the resistance of the tenants. Gladstone, the club of state terror in one hand, was forced to adopt a more gentle approach with the other – the granting of concessions in order to scrape from under the feet of the Land League the fertile soil in which it flourished.

In 1881, at the height of the land agitation, a second Land Act was introduced. This limited the power of the landlords to arbitrarily fix rents and established rent tribunals to which both the landlord and the tenant could appeal if they considered the rent unfair. Like the 1870 Act this reform merely rearranged slightly the relationship between the landlord and tenant, and avoided the real question: who owns the soil? In fact, because of rent arrears and other factors, over half the tenants with land over one acre were excluded from the provisions of this new Act.

Nevertheless the measure was sufficient temporarily to defuse the land agitation. After 1881 the Land League was in disarray. With its decline, the initiative in the struggle switched from the downtrodden masses in Ireland to the austere chambers in Westminster, where Charles Stewart Parnell was leading his Irish campaign of parliamentary disruption. Revolutionary action was supplanted by mere parliamentarianism. Social demands gave way to parliamentary rhetoric. Rather than being pounded by the hammer of land agitation, the bosses found themselves tickled by the feather of parliamentary intrigue.

However, the success scored by the Liberals did not impress the British Tory Party. In words at least they responded to even the faintest trace of concession to the tenants with frenzy. In 1885 Gladstone's Liberal administration was toppled and the Tories, under Lord Salisbury, came to power. Their answer to the Irish problem came close, in words at least, to the "solution" mooted during the Elizabethan era of "physical extermination". Lord Salisbury advocated that Ireland be held in total subjugation for twenty years until "her spirit is broken". After that time she "would be prepared to accept any gifts by way of local government, or repeal of the Coercion Laws, that you may be prepared to give her." In other words, when the very thought of rebellion had been hacked from the minds of the people they would be ready for concessions – and not until then.

All of the age-old policies of British imperialism came to the minds of the Tories during this election campaign and after. In 1886, distressed at their lack of organisation in Ireland during the previous election, concerned with etching out for himself a meteoric rise to prominence in the Tory Party, and seeing that the issue of Home Rule might suit its purpose, Lord Randolph Churchill visited Belfast and pronounced his "Orange card". If the policy of "divide and rule" had been good enough to suit his class in the past, it would be good enough to suit Tory interests in the present. In February 1886 he wrote:

> "I decided sometime ago that if the G.O.M. (Gladstone) went for Home Rule, the Orange card would be the one to play. Please God may it turn out to be the ace of trumps and not the 2."

It did! Lord Randolph was rewarded in the summer of 1886 with some of the worst sectarian rioting suffered by the people of Belfast for many years. The battle of words between the two parties who both represented the same fundamental class interests in Britain was a symptom of the switch in the policy of capital. Every class in society is divided into strata, some representing its forward-looking sections, others reflecting the outworn prejudices of past ages. Within the working class there are those who are conscious of their class identity and purpose, but there are also some whose minds are clogged with prejudices and reactionary ideas bestowed on them by capitalism. So too with the bourgeoisie. It too contains its rival factions and opinions. Every major crisis within society shatters the apparent unity of the dominant class and opens divisions for all to see. So the transformation of attitudes at the end of the nineteenth century on the issue of the land, and also, as will be explained later, on the issue of Home Rule, could not be a smooth or uniform process.

There are historical accounts which portray the struggle in Ireland in this period as a consequence of a war being conducted in the chambers of parliament between the Liberal and Tory parties. Such accounts explain nothing. Both the Liberals and the Tories in the final analysis served their class masters.

The Liberals, leaning on their support among the rising bourgeoisie, vied with their Tory and more aristocratic opponents to become the major and predominant party of capital. Both can accurately be described as capitalist parties. But a party of the ruling class can make statements which in concrete circumstances are against the interests of capital. At such times the pressures of the tops of society will be brought to bear on these political representatives to bring them to heel. Thus, despite the divisions in words between the Liberals and the Tories, in the last analysis, throughout this period, they were brought back to the fold of the bosses and forced to carry out the dictates of their masters.

On every major question the position of the leadership, of both the Liberal and the Tory parties, when spelt out in action as opposed to pure rhetoric, was the same. On the land, on Home Rule, on the need for coercion, this was to be shown.

Neither party was prepared to release fully the knife of repression as a means of subduing any movement of social agitation in Ireland. But both Tory and Liberal governments, up to and after the turn of the century, placed an ever greater emphasis on the use of concession both on the issue of land and on the issue of Home Rule.

A series of Land Acts was introduced to follow on from where those of 1870 and 1881 had left off. Land reform went through parliament again in 1887, 1891, 1896, 1903 and 1909. Of all these measures it was the Wyndham Act of 1903 which went furthest to resolve for the time being the land question. This Act permitted the tenant to buy the land. In the first five years after it received the royal assent, 228,958 tenants signed agreements for the purchase of their lands.

For their part the landlords were not particularly upset. With more than generous compensation terms, which would mean tenants owing them annuities for many years, they were not too concerned at the loss of their properties. A socially useless breed who had lived off the wealth produced by their tenants, they were content to live out their lives of idleness as comfortably as ever, but without the burden of "quarrelsome Irish peasants" to contend with.

The 1903 Act, only slightly amended in 1909, was introduced not by the Liberals but by the Tories. A.J. Balfour was Prime Minister at the time, the A.J. Balfour who had been appointed Irish Chief Secretary in 1895 by none other than Lord "twenty years of repression" Salisbury.

As with the issue of the land, so with the issue of Home Rule. Throughout the nineteenth century the fight for independence was inexorably linked with the struggle for ownership of the soil. In countries where there exists a vestige of landlordism or serfdom, there also exists an unquenchable yearning on the part of the tenants and peasants to own the land they work. In Ireland the masses of the rural population were not driven to seek independence because in their minds there existed some mystical conception of "the nation". In the minds of many of their leaders there existed such an idea, but the minds of the peasants, the landless and rootless poor, and of the tenant farmers contained more. They envisaged a nation in which the land would be theirs and the fruits of their labour would not be sent to parasitic absentee landlords. The struggles of such movements as Young Ireland and Fenianism were met with the full ferocity of state repression precisely because at bottom these were social movements against the class system of landlordism.

If the problem of the land could be resolved, the poison would be removed from the sting of the Home Rule demand. Just as with land reform, why should the capitalists stand four-square against Home Rule if their economic and military interests were not directly threatened? Without the danger of a social explosion accompanying any measure of autonomy there existed no reason why an Irish parliament with a few limited powers outside of defence and control of the ports could not be granted as a sop to the Irish. Quite the reverse. In fact the granting of a measure of autonomy would be a means of partially satisfying the call for independence and reducing the prospect of any real movement for genuine self-government emerging.

The switch of focus from the agitation of the Land League to the parliamentary campaign of Parnell in the early 1880s was symbolic of a transformation taking place – the separation of the Home Rule issue from the social issues which had driven the Irish masses into a succession of revolts.

Parnell replaced the moderate and ineffective Isaac Butt as Secretary of the Home Rule Confederation of Great Britain in 1877. During the land war he fought alongside Davitt, but utterly lacked the latter's revolutionary intent. Towards the end of this campaign Parnell was arrested. Before going to prison he contentedly assured his mistress, Kathleen O'Shea, that he was not concerned about his arrest because he knew that in a few months the agitation would be over. Then he could emerge a martyr from his jail and turn the defeats of the Land League into parliamentary victories for himself and his followers.

And indeed the exhaustion of the Land League allowed Parnell to have his way. Before the end of 1882 the Land League was replaced by a new organisation, the Irish National League. This body, unlike its predecessor, was dominated by the parliamentary party and concentrated its efforts on the issue of Home Rule.

In parliament Parnell successfully and skilfully used every major disruptive tactic at his disposal. A thorn in the side of the major parties, mainly because he was on occasions able to hold the balance of power, he was capable of focusing attention on the Home Rule issue. However, it had been the might of the Irish masses and the possibility of their establishing links with the working masses in the slums of the English cities which the bosses had feared. Parnell was a nuisance, but, like anyone who comes to conceive of a struggle mainly in terms of parliamentary majorities and parliamentary trickery, he was on stage removed from the driving force of the social struggle in Ireland. During the land campaign such tactics had supplemented the social struggle. They were a development of the land agitation into the austere institution of parliament itself. After the collapse of the Land League a parliamentary struggle was substituted for a campaign to mobilise the Irish people.

Parnell was riper material for British capital to squeeze into compromise. With the pushing to the background of Davitt, the separation of the social struggle from the Home Rule agitation was begun. Davitt himself summed this up when he spoke of the replacement of the Land League by the National League, which he said was "the complete eclipse by a purely parliamentary substitute of what had been a semi-revolutionary organisation. It was in a sense the overthrow of a movement, the enthronement of a man, the replacing of nationalism by Parnellism." Under Parnell the social and national issues were drawn apart. After him this separation was taken to even greater extremes.

Davitt stands a giant when compared to Parnell. But Parnell himself was a giant when places alongside the reactionaries who attempted to step into his shoes: the Redmonds, the Griffiths and the other leaders of the national struggle who, while they expressed their hatred of British rule, much more openly and energetically expressed their hatred, contempt and absolute dread of the Irish working class.

Given a lull in the struggle on the land and the emergence of a breed of political leaders with whom it might be possible to strike a deal, the "horrors" associated with even limited independence diminished as far as the ruling class was concerned. In 1886 Gladstone had introduced the first Home Rule Bill. As already mentioned this measure gave rise to venomous opposition on the part of the Tory chiefs. They even went to the lengths of calling for armed resistance to Home Rule in Ulster. The Bill, introduced in April, was defeated in June. It had offered a mere pretence of independence. It hoped to stifle the real demand by offering only the shadow. An Irish executive would be established, but excluded from its authority would be defence, foreign policy, trade and navigation.

In 1893 a second Home Rule Bill was presented to parliament by Gladstone and smashed to pieces by the hammer of the House of Lords veto. As with the first Bill it offered the proposed Irish parliament only the most nominal rights of independence.

The strategy underlying these Bills was aptly summed up by the phrase which was commonly coined: "Killing Home Rule with kindness". Just as the Tories had initially denounced all land reform, so they allowed no chance to slip by to bemoan this equally "weak-kneed policy".

But, lo and behold, even the Tories by the end of the century were being awakened to the more sensitive needs of capital. All but the most stupid backwoodsmen were beginning to see that a separate Irish parliament with negligible powers might not present the dangers initially imagined. Just the opposite! Not to grant limited autonomy might provoke a movement for genuine Home Rule. After 1903, with the landlords pensioned off to idleness, and the social issue of ownership of the land settled for the time being, this attitude was undoubtedly strengthened.

Needless to say the change of heart of the masters did not go unnoticed among the pawns in Ulster. During the 1895 elections the heads of the Tory Party had leaned heavily upon the Irish Unionists to draw electoral support. In 1900 a leading article in a Dublin daily paper which echoed the views of the Irish Unionist Alliance reminded the Tories that in 1895 "Lord Salisbury and the Duke of Devonshire publicly thanked the Alliance for its services in helping to return that Government to power. In 1900 the representative of the Queen in Ireland refused to meet a deputation of the Alliance." The article postulates the reasons for such a snub:

> "One is that the Government conceives itself to have no further use for those Irish Unionists whose efforts turned the scale in its favour in 1895. Another reason is that, with an insight which does credit to its cunning, but infinite discredit to its honour, the Government sacrifices the Irish loyalist on the altar of his own loyalty."

And then the supreme irony! What policy are the Tories actually pursuing? Precisely that which they themselves (when it suited) had condemned as "weak-kneed liberalism". The Tory attitude, the article continues, "is a striking exposition of the rewards which await Irish loyalty under a Conservative administration and an astonishing proof of the extremes to which the government will go in pursuit of its policy of "killing Home Rule with kindness".

As late as 1910 the Tory leaders, who within a few years were to be beating the Orange drum louder than ever, met in a constitutional conference to discuss the formation of a coalition government which would include in its policy

Home Rule for Ireland. At that time F.E. Smith, later Lord Birkenhead, a man destined to become one of the closest accomplices of the Carsonite rebellion, declared that Home Rule was "as a dead quarrel for which neither the country nor the party cares a damn outside of Liverpool and London".

At the turn of the century and after, the ruling class was unifying firmly behind the policy of sops to the Home Rule movement and buying out the landed aristocracy. Yet so greatly had conditions changed by 1911-12, when the third Home Rule Bill was being brought before parliament, that the very mention of such a "monstrosity" was enough to swing the tops of society behind advocacy of coercion, sectarianism and violence. Instead of killing Home Rule with kindness, the bourgeoisie was moved to demand that Home Rule be strangled with bigotry.

Why such an apparent change of heart? As always the answer to such riddles, which remain a complete mystery to the bourgeois historians because to them the dialectics of the class struggle are a closed book, lies in the changing balance of class forces.

Part II

CHAPTER TWO

Labour Emerges

Having brushed the nuisance of the social struggle for the land off one side of the stage, the ruling class had barely time to pause and draw breath before the giant of labour entered from the opposite wing, bringing with it the social struggle for the ending of the system of class exploitation itself. The emergence of the working class as an independent force for the first time in history left not one thing "sacred". Every attitude, every policy previously adopted by the bosses, had to be retested in terms of its effect on the emerging labour movement.

During and after the 1880s in Britain the labour movement was transformed by the development of "new unionism". Previously unorganised sections of the working class – the unskilled – were drawn into the unions in an explosive struggle. In 1888 there was the famous strike of the match girls of Bryant and May who formed their own union as a result. One year later under the leadership of Will Thorne, the gas workers formed a union. 20,000 members joined in the short space of four months. 1889 was also the year of massive struggles involving the dockers of London and again resulting in an unprecedented spread of union organisation. The Dock, Wharf, Riverside and General Labourers' Union rapidly grew into a powerful body of 30,000 members. The membership of the old unions also expanded during this period. And significantly the trades council movement sprang into life. Between 1889 and 1891, sixty-two new trades councils were formed. The most downtrodden, the most oppressed sections of society, were being drawn into revolt. [12]

The result was a shaking out of the old crass ideas of cringing reformism which had installed themselves at the head of the workers' organisations. In Britain the development of the labour movement had brought in its wake an irresistible demand for the extension of the franchise and an end to the old corrupt system of parliamentary local elections. Unable to arrest the growth of the workers' movement, the most clear-sighted of the bourgeoisie had attempted to lean on its better-off sections and head the movement in the di-

---

[12.] *Trades councils are bodies which bring together representatives from different trade unions in a specific geographical area e.g. Belfast Trades Council is made up of representatives of trade union branches in Belfast.*

rection of reformism. Not the strength of capitalism but the narrow craft prejudices of the "labour aristocracy", as Marx termed them, allowed the private property system to survive.[13]

The development of "new unionism" introduced a new chapter of class militancy. The blunt ideas of opportunism of the old union tops were met with the checks, challenges and outright opposition of the newly unionised workers. Class conflict in society produced a battle of ideas within the labour organisations. Tom Mann, Ben Tillet and other new leaders emerged to take positions in the movement, displacing those who had peddled the narrow class-compromise views of the labour aristocracy. [14]

Capital would have to resort to new methods to restrain this new threat! If the workers could not be held back by the cushioning of their leaders and the development amongst them of soft ideas, then they would have to be met head on. The efforts of the bosses merely succeeded in channelling the struggle of the workers in another direction. Facing restrictions on their industrial activity, the movement turned eventually to political action. In 1892 the TUC drew up a scheme for a Labour Representation Board. A few independent Labour MPs had already entered parliament.

Further attacks from the bosses accelerated these developments. South Wales railway workers struck in 1900. The employers issued an injunction on the union for the picketing activities of its members. In 1901 the Taff Vale decision resulted in the union being asked to pay £23,000 damages to the company.

In this the state institutions were doing no more than playing their real role of guardians of capital. But by presenting this open face to the workers they gave the necessary impetus to the developing political consciousness of the movement. By 1903 the bulk of the unions had affiliated to the Labour Representation Committee. Between 1903 and 1905 affiliation to this body rose from 445,450 to 861,200. The most decisive and important step towards the breakup of the Liberal-Labour alliance had been taken.

The development of the Irish labour movement mirrored closely but not exactly that of Britain. Early Irish unions, representing the skilled workers in such industries as ship-building, the railways and the breweries, grew as part and parcel of the British movement. In fact many early British unions organised branches in Ireland, in part as a protection against surplus Irish labour being used against them in Britain. Twice during the nineteenth century the TUC emphasized this bond by meeting in Ireland.

[13.] *Labour aristocracy is a term sometimes used by Marxists to refer to the better-off skilled sections of the working class who were at this point organised in craft unions*

[14.] *Tom Mann and Ben Tillot were prominent English socialists and leading trade unionists who made a name for themselves as leaders of the London dock strike of 1889.*

The stirring of independent political action in Belfast coincided with the political growth of the movement in Britain. In 1891 delegates to the Belfast Trades Council called for a branch of the Labour Representation Committee to be set up in the city. Two years later a Belfast branch of the Independent Labour Party was formed. Trades council candidates stood in local elections in 1894 and again in 1898. However, the emergence of the "new unionism", the organisation of the unskilled, did not come until later.

Thus, while the drawing together of the political nucleus of Irish labour mirrored similar developments in Britain, it did so at a different pace. In Britain the infancy of the political consciousness of labour was reflected in the Liberal-Labour alliance. That infancy was shattered by the impetus of class struggle. In Ireland, precisely because of the delay in the rise of "new unionism", the movement remained bound by old ideologies for longer.

Reflecting the fact that a socialist consciousness even in Belfast was at little more than a foetus stage, the early spokesmen of the unions and the first political candidates to which they turned were both confused by, and filled with, the old reactionary ideologies from which the movement was attempting to break.

Alexander Bowman stood in Belfast in 1885 with the support of the Trades Council. He, at one time, had attempted to form a Protestant Home Rule Association and had been ejected from his trade-union office for doing so. Another of the founders of the political wing of the movement and a leading figure nationally was William Walker. Walker never managed to shake from his mind the traces of Unionism which marked this infantile stage of labour development. Like the movement itself, one part of Walker was groping towards a developed socialist stand, while the rest remained loyal to the political ideas of his masters. When the movement lurched forward Walker's Unionism got the better of his socialism and he ended up within the Unionist Party.

The rise of the Labour Party in Britain after 1903 had its immediate effects in Ireland. A conference of the Labour Representation Committee attended by trade-unionists and ILP members was held that year in Belfast. Also in 1903 a resolution was passed at the Irish Trade Union Congress calling for the creation of a pledge-bound Labour Party. But, unlike in England, where the struggle had developed to a higher level, this resolution was ignored. The activists and most advanced layers of the movement were drawn by the idea of labour representation even at this early stage. But the broad mass of the Irish workers had not had the whip of a Taff Vale cracked over their heads to drive them, as a class, towards independent political consciousness and political involvement. It was to take a further nine years and titanic struggles, North and South, before the Trade Union Congress was forced to put the flesh on the demand for an Irish Labour Party. Nonetheless, from the 1900s the entire movement drew itself forward towards the inevitable political activity.

The struggle to organise the unskilled may have come later in Ireland than in England. Old ideas may have held sway at the top of the movement for a few years after the English match girls, gas workers, dockers, etc., had discarded them. None-the-less when the battle calls were heard they ushered in a period of intense struggle which developed to a revolutionary pitch.

In the first decades of this century "new unionism" swept all before it in Ireland. It took the camps of Green Toryism and Orange Toryism and cracked them asunder. The north east was the main industrial centre in Ireland. There the people worked in slavish conditions, out of their sweat producing profits for the linen barons, the magnates of shipbuilding and engineering and for the other financiers and capitalists. It was in the north east that the revolt began. As early as the 1890s, election results had shown the beginnings of the fragmentation of the all-class alliance of the various Unionists and nationalists. In 1898 William Walker and six other representatives of Belfast Trades Council were elected to Belfast City Council.

At the turn of the century the Orange Order split. An Independent Orange Order was formed. Its leaders spent their energies denouncing the gentry who headed the Orange Order as being too soft towards the Catholics. The split was along class lines, with the bulk of the working-class members of the Orange Order moving behind the new Independent Orange Order, which was forced to echo the class aspirations of the Protestant workers within its ranks.

On 12th, July 1905, the Independent Orange Order produced a manifesto, part of which read:

> "In an Ireland in which Protestant and Roman Catholics stand sullen and discontent, it is not too much to hope that both will reconsider their positions and, in their common trials, unite on a true basis of nationality. The higher claims of our distracted country have been too long neglected in the strife of party and of creed."

In the elections of 1903 the Unionist establishment received a sharp blow. Sir James Craig presented himself to the electorate of North Fermanagh. The election was fought in the period immediately prior to the passing of the Wyndham Land Act of that year, Craig himself opposed by Edward Mitchell, who claimed to stand for the "people's cause against the landlords". By 200 votes Mitchell beat the man who was later to become a Prime Minister of the post-partition Northern Ireland state.

At first this rising tempo of class discontent found its expression in splits within the sectarian Tory groupings. Paradoxically, at times it even gave rise to more extreme variants of sectarianism. The magnetic attraction of the class movement first of all revealed itself in the breaking up of the old political patterns. Eventually its own clear lines of force were to become established.

In the 1906 general election the Unionist establishment was shown to be in disarray. An Independent won in South Belfast, a Nationalist captured the west of the city, and in North Belfast William Walker came within a few hundred votes of capturing a seat for Labour. The extent to which class issues and ideas were beginning to predominate is not always understood. Particularly this is so since the history books generally inform us that the first decades of this century were dominated by the debate over Home Rule. On the contrary! In 1905, 1906 and 1907 the grip of the bigots was all but broken in Belfast. Who better to confirm this than one of the architects of the loyalist reaction, the future gunrunner for Carson, F.H. Crawford. In a letter written in 1906 he lamented on behalf of his reactionary Unionist brethren,

"we have lost a lot of the staunch Unionist workmen in Belfast. They consider themselves betrayed by their leader Mr. Balfour and have gone for the labour and socialist programmes. This is what we have to combat locally. The old Unionist enthusiasm is dead among the masses here. These are facts and all in touch with the workingmen know it."

"The old Unionist enthusiasm is dead among the masses"! What could be clearer or more precise! Those who did not know this when Crawford penned these words were soon to learn it. In 1907 the Irish working class signalled for the first time that they had arrived on the scene of history. "New unionism", when it spread to Belfast, wrote out again, this time in the vivid language of class struggle, Crawford's statement that the workingmen "have gone for the labour and socialist programme".

In 1907 James Larkin came to Belfast from Liverpool as a full-time organiser of the National Union of Dock Labourers. Very quickly he drew the majority of the dockers into membership, easily displacing the less militant Carter's Association. In June 1907 Larkin called out 500 dockers in support of a wage claim. This was the small beginning of a titanic clash which was to propel the young proletariat of Belfast into head-on collision with the state and the bosses. A few weeks after the beginning of the dockers' struggle, the carters came out in sympathy and with their own demands for improved pay and for a closed shop. The movement developed and spread. By the end of July 500 dockers, 1000 carters and 1000 coalmen, who also struck in sympathy, were involved in the battle.

Feeding on the miserable conditions of industrial Belfast, the strike movement had taken root. Symptomatic of the support among wide layers of society for the strikers was the response of the police. Larkin had made an appeal to the members of the Royal Irish Constabulary in Belfast on the basis of the hours they were being forced to work. The result was a police mutiny which was eventually suppressed, most of the Belfast police finding themselves transferred to country areas where the "seditious" propaganda of Larkin and his like would not reach them, and where they would be rubbing shoulders with the rural population, not with workers. 6000 troops were drafted into Belfast, supposedly to protect "life and property".

"Property" the troops were sent to protect. "Life" they were not! In August, during rioting on the Falls Road, the army opened fire and shot dead two men. These riots were part and parcel of a desperate attempt on the part of the bosses to divide the workers along sectarian lines. Protestant bigots pointed to Larkin in an attempt to brand the whole dispute as a "plot by the nationalists". The attacks by the troops took place on the Falls Road in order that the rioting would appear to be sectarian and that the real issues could be disguised. Towards the end of the dispute, F.H. Crawford commented on the August riots in a letter to a Major Doyne of Wexford:

"What a blessing all the rioting took place in a Catholic quarter of the city. This branded the whole thing as a nationalist movement."

The development of sectarianism was prevented partly as a result of the prompt intervention of the strike leaders. A notice was issued by the strike committee after the August riots. It read:

"not as Catholics or Protestants, as nationalists or unionists, but as Belfast men and workers, stand together and don't be misled by the employers' game of dividing Catholic and Protestant."

Sectarianism could not take root because the conditions for it were not ripe. On July 12, 1907, two separate Orange parades were held in Belfast while the industrial battle was being fought out all around. One of these parades was organised by the Independent Orange Order. Not only did this parade pass a resolution supporting Larkin and the strikers, but a collection in aid of the strike fund was also taken up.

In August the carters returned to work having won on the question of wages but failed to secure the closed shop. Later the coalmen returned on similar terms. The dockers stuck it out until the beginning of November, when they could stay out no longer, and they returned to work partially defeated. In November further unrest spread, and carters, cranemen and coalmen struck, complaining that the August agreement was not being implemented by the employers. The British union leadership intervened over the heads of Larkin and the local leaders. The men were persuaded to return to work.

This unforgettable struggle opened a new chapter in Irish history. The law of history etched out during the land agitation of the previous century that, when social issues are presented to the forefront, all other issues, including sectarianism, can be seen to melt. The land struggles, the movement of the United Irishmen and other such movements had forged a unity of Catholic and Protestant. The emergence of the industrial working class once again showed that sectarianism could be overcome. But the class movement begun in 1907 did not merely repeat the history of past solidarity. All history is a development. The working class in 1907 raised the concept of the unity of Catholic and Protestant to a higher-than-ever level. The workers proved more deeply than ever that, when the class struggle is going forward, nothing, not even the most vicious attempts to scar it with bigotry, can stand in its path.

Even Crawford, surveying the attempts by his class to restore their authority during the strike, had to admit defeat. To him the strike was led by nationalists, but "the serious part of the business is that they have duped a lot of Protestants, who call themselves Independent Orangemen, and a few demagogues who like to hear their own voice."

Belfast 1907 was a prelude to even stormier developments in the South. The disgust felt by Larkin at the activities of Sexton and the national leaders of the dockers' union resulted in a split. In 1908 Larkin formed the Irish Transport and General Workers' Union. The split did not assist the development of the movement in the North. Few joined Larkin's union. The revolutionary socialist James Connolly, who was later appointed by Larkin as Northern organiser of the Irish Transport and General Workers' Union (ITGWU), on a number of occasions reacted strongly to criticism from Larkin that he was failing to make significant headway with the union membership in the North. Connolly explained that the conditions in the North after 1907 were not as easy as those in the period immediately before the strike. The workers were pausing to catch their breath. In these conditions the split in the union was a negative setback.

While the struggle in the North temporarily ebbed, the formation of the ITGWU heralded a series of class battles throughout the rest of the country, which culminated in the 1913 Dublin lockout. The growth of the ITGWU was a barometer of the explosive developments building up. In 1911 they had approximately 4000 members. By 1913 its numbers had swelled to 300,000. A paper produced by Larkin, The Irish Worker, began in 1911 with a circulation of 15,000 copies. This very quickly rose, and levelled off at a weekly distribution of 20,000. By contrast, at the same time, the newspaper of Sinn Féin sold a mere 2000 copies. Such figures give a true indication of the balance of class forces.

The mood within society was again apparent from the attitude of those within the ruling circles. In 1911, referring to the strike of railway workers, the head of the Dublin Chamber of Commerce pronounced:

"This strike is not a strike in the ordinary sense of the word: it is the beginning of a social war, a revolution... the thin edge of the wedge of socialism... force must be met with force and the union of the workers must be met by unions of the employers to uphold public order."

Such sentiments were not isolated. The employers, for their part, reacted to the growth of trade unionism, and in particular to the use by the Larkinites of the crippling weapon of the sympathy strike, by organizing an Employers' Federation. One of the leading Dublin capitalists, a man called William Martin Murphy, less politely described by Larkin as a "modern capitalist vampire", who made a career of "destroying the characters of men who he was and is not fit to be a doormat for", organised 4000 employers into this "strike-breaking" Federation. With this the battle lines were clearly drawn.

Strikes in Dublin, in the Jacobs Factory, among seamen, among firemen, on the port and a sympathy strike by 16,000 railwaymen who downed tools in solidarity with 200,000 British rail workers then on strike, were the beginnings of the class war. In August 1911 the employers locked out 550 members of the Irish Transport and General Workers' Union in Wexford, demanding that they leave this union. During this struggle, which lasted until February 1912, the workers went so far as to organise their own defence, through the establishment of a workers' police force. Connolly was called in to organise the strike. Ultimately a compromise was reached. A new union was formed for the locked-out men and in the event this soon merged with the ITGWU.

Wexford was but a dress rehearsal for a concrete offensive by the employers in an attempt to break the ITGWU and with it destroy the combativity of the young Irish proletariat. This offensive reached its crescendo when in August 1913 Murphy and his Employers' Federation declared war on the workers of Dublin. ITGWU members working for Murphy's newspaper, the Irish Independent, were told that they must resign their union membership or lose their jobs. The paper was blacked by the union and the men were locked out.[15]

By late August the use of the lockout tactic had spread as other employers expressed their "class solidarity". By September 25,000 workers were locked out. Each had received a document to sign stating that they would have nothing to do with Larkin's union. As quickly as the workers refused, the employers locked the gates.

Friedrich Engels said that the state, in the final analysis, could be reduced to "armed bodies of men acting in defence of property". No worker who has been involved in industrial action and has been met with the fury of the media, the police, army, courts, etc., will need these words to be explained. Dublin in 1913 presented a crystal-clear picture of the true role of the capitalist state. All the instruments of repression available were swung into action on the side of the bosses. The strike leaders, including Connolly and Larkin, were arrested. Strike meetings were banned and the police used to break up or attempt to break up any that were held.

If the forces of the state are in the hands of the bosses, then the workers have nowhere to look for protection except to themselves. The workers of Dublin learned this simple lesson in 1913. When a workers' band was threatened by police attack, the workers formed a defence guard to protect it. Initially these workers carried hurley sticks to defend themselves. It was from such incidents that the Irish Citizen Army, the first army of the working class in Ireland, was formed. James Connolly, one of its founders, wrote: "an armed organisation of the Irish working class is a phenomenon new in Ireland. Hitherto the workers of Ireland have fought as parts of the armies led by their masters, never as members of an army officer, trained and inspired by men of their own class. Now, with arms in their hands, they propose to steer their own course, to carve their own futures."

In addition to the official state institutions, its semi-official bodies unleashed their venom on the heads of the strikers. The church hierarchy, the

---

[15] *'Blacking' is when workers refuse to handle goods from or bound for a particular company or place.*

barons of the press, and with them the right-wing leaders of Irish nationalism, combined with the rest of "respectable society" to shower abuse on the mighty army of labour which had emerged from the slums and had brought the city to a virtual standstill. Nationalist leaders such as Arthur Griffith showed their true colours. Griffith is reported to have advocated that the best way of getting the workers back to their work would be to bayonet the leaders!

But nothing could have matched the role of the church hierarchy. Trade unionists in Britain offered to foster some of the starving children of the Dublin strikers until the dispute was over. The "holy" priests of Dublin would have none of this. Gangs of "godly" people were organised to picket the docks to prevent Catholic children being shipped to the homes of Protestants and atheists. Better, in the minds of these clerical bigots that the children starve but remain true to the "faith of their fathers" than they should fill their stomachs with Protestant food. Arthur Griffith's Sinn Féin backed the antics of the clerics with the following piece of cynicism: "it has recently been discovered that the Irish working man is not an Irish working man at all. He is a unit of humanity, a human label of internationalism, a brother of the men over the water who rule his country."

Every great class movement simplifies and clarifies class relationships. It divides society into camps cutting to the root of religious and other reactionary propaganda which serve to camouflage the real nature of capitalism. Dublin in 1913 was divided into what Sinn Féin described in horrified but nevertheless correct terms as the "units of humanity", that is the workers who owned no part of Ireland, and the privileged class and the owners of property who were fighting to hold onto their privileges.

Just as the 1907 dispute sundered the Unionist alliance, so the nationalists were pulled apart by the Dublin lockout. Within a nationalist or a republican all-class alliance there are those whose sights are on a socialist republic and others whose minds are filled with the vision of a capitalist republic or nation – with themselves in charge, of course! These strands are always separated by the pull of the class struggle. In 1910 the left wing of Sinn Féin split off to form a movement called "Irish Freedom". Again in 1913 the left of the republican movement were drawn to the workers, while those of Griffith's ilk stood with the employers. Those republicans who were later to lead the 1916 insurrection in Dublin stood apart from their right-wing associates by the support they gave in 1913 to the workers.

In the event, neither side won a conclusive victory. The workers of Dublin struggled on until February 1914. Then they were starved back to work. They had not won. But neither had the bosses. The union had not been broken. The workers had fought the issue to a standstill, until they could fight no more. They could have won, but only with the active support of the British trade-union movement. Throughout the strike British workers had given enormous support. In September the TUC voted £5000 in assistance. The miners voted £1000 per week in October. One member of the Dublin lockout committee claimed that £150,000 was donated to assist their struggle. However, the crucial issue lay in extending this support to a total blacking of Dublin goods and even sympathetic strikes in England which would have hit hard at the pockets of people like Murphy who had, for example, sizeable investments in the tramways of many British cities. The TUC leaders drew back from such a development of their support for the Dublin workers. Many of them also feared that to go further in support of the strike would give a boost to what to them were the dangerous ideas of Connolly and Larkin.

A special Trade Union Congress held in December overwhelmingly defeated a motion which asked the British transport workers not to handle Dublin goods. Together the British and Irish workers held the head of Dublin capital in a noose. But instead of tightening their grip the British leaders drew back. As the support from Britain dwindled the Dublin workers were forced into retreat. Between 1907 and 1914 the Irish working class for the first time in history flexed their muscles and fought as an independent force in pursuit of their own demands. They did not win, but neither did they suffer a humiliating defeat. Instead they came to see in action the tremendous power they possessed and to understand how that power must be utilized and deployed in future struggles.

Such industrial militancy in the last analysis must find its reflection in the political outlook of the movement. Although later than in Britain, the ideas of class harmony of the old-style trade unionism were shattered more completely, more forcibly in Ireland. In the first decades of this century the cradle of the movement had been in Belfast. There the shades of the future were fought out in the form of the battle of ideas of James Connolly and William Walker.

The Connolly-Walker controversy was more than a war of words between two individuals, albeit important individuals in the movement. Connolly's approach echoed the revolutionary stirrings of the masses, while Walker gave expression to the more conservative and inert layers of the movement. Walker's "Labour Unionism" in effect meant the containment of the workers' movement within the bounds of sectarianism. Connolly, although he was incorrect in arguing for the complete separation of the Irish from the British movement, represented the need for independent and united political action by the working class.

Before the dockers, carters and the unskilled showed that they were a force to be reckoned with, Walker-type views predominated. Connolly managed to gain the support of only a tiny handful. His Irish Socialist Republican Party, which he formed in Belfast in 1897, never had a total membership of more than 100. But Connolly stood on the side of historical development while Walker came more and more into conflict with it. The Irish Trade Union Congress, established in 1894, was transformed by the explosions which marked the growth of new unionism. In 1912 the need for independent political action, which had been accepted in words in 1903, was re-emphasized. Connolly, recognizing the need for a mass party of the workers, particularly in the light of the developing crisis over Home Rule in the North, moved a resolution calling for the establishment of a Labour Party. It is noteworthy, especially because of the attitude of some of those who pretend to follow Connolly today, that he moved that the union form a broadly based Labour Party, despite the fact that he had built up a small socialist party and that other assortments of independent political parties which claimed to represent the workers then existed. Connolly was free of the haughty political sectarianism which prompts small socialist groups today to embellish their organisations with the pompous and ambitious title of the organisation of the working class.

In 1912 the process of establishing a Labour Party was boosted by the decision of the ITUC to change its title to the Irish Trade Union Congress and Labour Party. This decision was taken again on a motion moved by Connolly which was passed by 49 votes to 18. Signalling the transformation of the outlook of the movement was the adoption of the view that "labour unrest can only be ended by the abolition of the capitalist system".

The immediate pre-war period in Britain also ushered in a new wave of major strikes. Railwaymen, dockers, seamen and miners all participated in major and prolonged disputes. Within the unions and the Labour Party a new layer of younger and more militant workers were clamouring for more decisive action on the part of their leaders. Between 1907 and 1912 almost every section of the British working class was involved in strike action. During these years the number of days lost due to strikes increased from 1,878,679 to 38,142,101. Not the question of Home Rule for Ireland, but the profound and revolutionary implications of such figures, and the discontent that they revealed, were the prime concern of the British ruling class during these years. Without understanding this there can be no understanding of the subsequent course of Irish history. Unionism, nationalism, Carsonism, Redmondism – all these phenomena can be explained only in the context of the social agitation then developing.

Before 1903 the British bosses had looked to the land issue as their major threat in Ireland. They feared that it might act as a fillip to the English workers. So the land agitation was largely dissolved with the tonic of concession.

But the struggle ebbed only to find its feet on a higher level. After 1907 the bosses feared, not the prospect of a unity of English workers with Irish tenants, but of the workers of Belfast and Dublin with their brothers in the mines, docks and factories of Britain.

Such struggles, such fears on the part of the ruling class, form the real backcloth to the Home Rule crisis in the period before the First World War. Only by picturing clearly the momentous significance of this tumultuous birth of Irish labour can the attitude of the bosses, the Liberals, Tories and nationalists, and the fears of sections of the workers, be understood. Without the clarity of class analysis we are left to retreat to the mumbo-jumbo of "holy wars" and tribal "tom toms" contained in too many historical accounts. To attempt an analysis of the events of the Home Rule agitation, without beginning from the conditions of the class struggle both in Ireland and in Britain, would be like attempting to paint and decorate a house before it is built.

In 1910 a general election left the Irish Parliamentary Party with the balance of power in the House of Commons. The result was a deadlock and another general election which merely re-created the deadlock. Home Rule was thus a major issue. Two years later, on the 11th of April, 1912, the third Home Rule Bill was introduced by the Liberal government.

On this occasion a crisis developed which made the events surrounding the defeats of the previous Home Rule Bill appear like minor ripples in a stormy ocean. Several factors had changed by 1912. First the unquenchable thirst of the working class for democratization of the parliamentary procedure had forced through in 1911 a Parliament Act which limited the veto of the House of Lords. In future the Lords could delay a measure only three times in any one parliamentary session. After that a Bill would become law without the aristocratic blessing of the members of the upper chamber.

The neat constitutional method of defeating Home Rule was therefore blocked. But this in itself was not the decisive question. The threat from the working-class movement was. In the immediate post-war period the British ruling class was struck with dread of a social revolution at home. Faced with strike after strike affecting every major industry, with the suffragette movement and the attacks on that sacred institution the House of Lords, they trembled for the very existence of their system. In this period the British ruling class was preparing for a physical confrontation with the forces of the labour movement. To concede Home Rule in Ireland would only inflame the situation by opening the way to the prospect of a socialist Ireland with all the repercussions that could have in Britain. [16]

Hence those who had previously adopted a soft attitude, even to Home Rule, began to move in the opposite direction. In the immediate pre-war period, capital was moving from its position of concession to the Irish struggle to a policy of coercion and of encouragement of sectarianism in order both to prevent Home Rule, and also to shatter the solidarity of the labour movement. Immediately the development of an armed movement of revolt among the Unionists in Ireland, particularly those in the North, was developed and encouraged by the British ruling class. It was hoped that the club of sectarianism could be used to shatter both Home Rule and also the greater threat of workers' unity.

This change in position had the effect once again of pulling apart the Tory and Liberal parliamentary parties. History was being repeated by the course of transforming past relationships into their reverse. Previously the Tories had found themselves out of tune with the demands of their paymasters. Increasingly now it was the Liberals who discovered that their message was not the one which the capitalists wished to hear.

Liberal support for Home Rule was maintained right up until 1914, although amendments, including the question of a temporary partition, were considered. The Liberal leaders grew more and more out of touch with the existing mood within the top circles of society including the army. In 1914 a private secretary with knowledge of the attitudes of the Liberal leaders explained their plans to the Unionist Edward Carson:

> "the plan is to procrastinate until the patience of the hooligan element in Belfast is exhausted and they begin to riot and incidentally you and the loyalists... Mr. Lloyd George is the only one who does not think things are serious. He said casually over the tea table, 'put the Crimes Act in force, and the whole thing will fizzle out in a week'."

This would have been all very well but for the attitudes of the army chiefs! While the Liberals were destroying the loyalist movement over cups of tea in London, the generals, the capitalists and the landowners were giving it every assistance and encouragement in Belfast. In March 1914 army regiments based at the Curragh camp in the South were ordered on "manoeuvres" to

---

[16]. *Suffragettes were the militant movement which fought for women's right to vote*

the North. Fifty officers promptly mutinied rather than carry out their instructions. Lloyd George and his colleagues soon realized that the "loyalist rebellion" would not be snuffed out in a week, not because of the strength of Carson's forces, but because the ruling circles of society on whom the Liberals, just as much as the Tories, depended, did not want it. The government found itself suspended in mid-air, a group of legislators rapidly losing their power to administer what they might choose to enact.

In vain will pro-capitalist writers attempt to paint this "forgotten episode in British history" of the Curragh mutiny as the action of a few junior officers. The revolt was a revolt of the heads of society. The Curragh mutiny was prepared for and received, the consent of the ruling class and the Tory leaders. Secret meetings between the Liberal cabinet and the tops of the army did not remain secret, because the army heads promptly passed on all information of Liberal plans to their Tory allies. In November 1913 the Tory leader Bonar Law, at a meeting in Dublin, had announced that the army would mutiny if sent to Ulster. Carson around this time was able confidently to predict that if the people of England allowed the government to attempt to coerce Ulster "the British army could not stand the strain".

In this there is a profound lesson which the labour movement should take to heart for all time. The British ruling class is fond of presenting itself to the world as the champions of democracy. The years 1911-14 give insight into the real contempt the bourgeoisie has for parliament. Democratic rule, the right of free speech, the right to elect governments: these are acceptable so long as they do not challenge the class basis of society. In fact they provide the most stable basis of capitalist rule.

But when the antics of parliamentary leaders, even of Prime ministers, step beyond that which the real rulers, the capitalist class, consider to be acceptable bounds, these people, even the institute of parliament itself, become "expendable".

1907 dockers' and carters' strike marks the development of a new chapter in the history of the labour movement on this island

1913 lockout stands out as an important battle between the Dublin working class and their bosses

In 1918, a general strike successfully prevented the British ruling class from conscripting 150,000 men

This period saw countless example of workers organising 'soviets', most famously the Limerick Soviet

BELFAST MUNICIPAL ELECTIONS.

15th JANUARY, 1920.

SHANKILL DIVISION.

VOTE FOR

Gordon, Kyle & M'Williams

Labour movement candidates were elected in every part of Belfast in the 1920 local elections, including topping the poll in areas such as the Shankill

DAWSON GORDON
Nominee of Flax Roughers
and Textile Workers.

SAM KYLE
Nominee of I.L.P.

ROBERT M'WILLIAMS
Nominee of I.L.P.

The Official Labour Candidates

NOTE:—The only Official Labour Candidates are those endorsed by the

BELFAST LABOUR PARTY.

Published by the Belfast Labour Representation Committee.
and Printed by Thos. Brough & Cox, Donegall St., Belfast.

1920 saw vicious sectarian pogroms and expulsions from the shipyard of Catholic workers and labour movement activists.

CHAPTER THREE

Capital Revolts

I n 1912 the Tory leader, Bonar Law, who had earlier been prepared to accept Home Rule, bluntly exposed his attitude to parliament and to democracy when he threatened:

> "If Ulster is earnest, if Ulster does resist by force there are stronger things than parliamentary majorities... the government which gave an order to employ troops for that purpose (enforced Home Rule) would run the risk of being lynched in London."

Fine words from a man whose class fifty years later could jail two building workers at Shrewsbury for conspiracy for the crime of picketing! Within Ireland the anti-Home-Rule agitation took shape in the period of the first Home Rule bill, mainly as a reactionary movement headed by the aristocracy. Lords and ladies of "esteem", traditionally supporters of the Conservatives, were the most prominent members in the Irish Loyal and Patriotic Union formed in May 1885. These people denounced the "communistic crew" who backed Parnell. Correctly they summed up the dangers of Home Rule to their social position by stating that Parnell's support "consists of the lowest half of the population: of tenant farmers, on a small scale, who aim at acquiring the ownership of the soil they till without the usual preliminary of paying for it, of labourers who covet the land of the farmers."

Paradoxically the place where Unionism sank its deepest roots began as its weakest area. The ILPU gathered its support from the landowning aristocracy and was strongest in the South. However, it remained an aristocratic movement. In 1891 it was supplanted by the Irish Unionist Alliance, which drew its support from the Southern landowners. After 1903 the stake of this class in anti-Home-Rule agitation was loosened. Unionism in the South sank into relative impotence, a fact emphasized in 1917 at the Irish Convention convened by Lloyd George when the Irish Unionist Alliance was arguing vehemently against partition, posing the alternative of an all-

Ireland parliament which could provide safeguards for the Unionists. When the first Home Rule Bill was introduced the Liberals were split on the issue; sections of the business community of Ireland who had been Liberals moved to a "Liberal Unionist" stance, and eventually switched their allegiance to the Tories.

Contrary to the impression which has often been given, the development of a "Unionist" outlook was not confined to the businessmen in the North. Throughout the country the large capitalists, as for example the Guinness family, together with the big ranchers, supported the maintenance of the link with Britain. However, because the bulk of large-scale industry was concentrated in the north east, the strongest base for this reaction among the business community existed in that area.

Throughout the nineteenth century the development of capitalism in Ireland has been uneven. The linen industry in the North was able to attract capital for investment. At the same time it was not decimated by the English economy because it was not in competition with the products of the British capitalists. Under Free Trade, linen prospered. By the first decade of the twentieth century there were more linen mills in Belfast than in any other country.

Parallel with, and as a result of, the spectacular growth in linen came an equally spectacular growth in the engineering industry as firms developed to produce machinery for use in the mills. All took place in step with the growth of the major industrial centres in Britain. Ease of access to the British boosted the development of Belfast as part of an industrial triangle whose other points were Liverpool and Glasgow. As in both those cities, shipbuilding became a major industry in Belfast. Its two shipyards, Harland and Wolfe and Workman Clarke and Co., were major enterprises by international standards.

The growth of a nationalist movement demanding protection for Irish industry bent the big bourgeoisie, especially in the North, in the direction of Unionism. The prospect of tariff barriers being erected between them and the major sources of raw materials in Britain and elsewhere horrified the owners of large-scale enterprises whose production was often geared to export. After the first Home Rule Bill many switched their allegiance from the Liberals to the Tories. They allied themselves with the aristocrats in the Unionist Clubs movement of the late nineteenth century. In 1904 an Ulster Unionist Council was formed and again the support of the business community was given to its activities.

Big business was prepared to give its backing to the Unionist movement and lend support to attempts to whip up sectarianism which took place during the first debates over Home Rule. After the 1907 strike and faced with the spectacle of an enraged working class, their commitment, financial and otherwise, to the loyalists grew beyond all proportion. Like growing sections of the British ruling class they were moved to desperate lengths in order to safeguard their property and their system.

In 1911 the reactionary Dublin lawyer, Sir Edward Carson, who had made his name defending landlords in the courts, and who was selected as the "guru" of the Unionist cause, was induced to threaten to establish a provisional government in Ulster if Home Rule became a reality. His threat was designed to destroy Home Rule as a whole, not to bring about partition. In 1913 Ulster Unionists even went so far as to select the personnel for such a government. These steps were supported by the British Tories, by all backwoodsmen of empire-building British imperialism, but also by growing sections of the bourgeoisie in Britain together with the Ulster business community. [17]

With such backing, funds proved no problem. In fact the way in which the bank balance of the Carsonites swelled almost overnight gives an indication of the attitudes of the tops of society. In 1913 an Ulster Volunteer Force (UVF) was formed. A special Carson Defence Fund was set up so that the accounts of the Ulster Unionist Council would remain presentable to the Inland Revenue. The Ulster Unionist Council showed an annual expenditure in the region of £1000. Meanwhile tens of thousands were pumped into the reserves of the UVF, to supply arms, to drill and to train volunteers, to issue propaganda etc. In one meeting called to set up a fund, a quarter of a million pounds was pledged. Most gave donations in the region of £10,000. Within one week £387,000 had been promised and in the short space of four months donations to the tune of £1,000,000 were either promised or made.

From Britain and even further afield the donations poured in. Lord Rothschild presented a mere £10,000. Lord Iveagh and the Duke of Bedford reduced their fortunes by a similar amount. The poet of "empire" Rudyard Kipling handed over a mere £30,000! Such sums marked the "class solidarity" of the bosses. [18]

Carson's activities and those of the UVF have been well documented. In 1912 400,000 people signed the "Covenant" which was a pledge to resist Home Rule. In 1914 25,000 guns were secretly smuggled into Larne on the Clyde Valley. The town was taken over by the UVF and the guns distributed in carloads throughout the province.

To these activities, to the open marching and drilling of these armed volunteers, the state forces closed their eyes. From this the question must be posed: what would have happened if the workers of Ireland had attempted to

---

[17.] Edward Carson also made a name for himself in prosecuting Oscar Wilde for his homosexuality.
[18.] According to the Bank of England's "inflation calculator", that £1 million is the equivalent of £116 million today.

import guns and tried to take over a town for that purpose? There would have been mass arrests and widespread searches. Yet Larne was surrendered to the UVF without a shot being fired. The state forces were supposed to be fully occupied with a few diversionary incidents in Belfast! Then a few haystacks here and there may have been turned over in the hope that one or two of the 25,000 rifles might be found! That was the extent to which the Clyde Valley incident annoyed the bosses.

The British ruling class was prepared to wage a ruthless war on the workers of Dublin. It was prepared to send its army against the miners of South Wales, with no squeals of horror or threats of mutiny from the officer class whenever bayonets were drawn at Tonypandy in 1910 – but Ulster, they declared, "must not be coerced". In reality the government was paralyzed and could not move against the UVF simply because the real forces of the state, the army and the police, the business community, etc., were firmly on the side of the loyalists. The most vicious sectarianism was being invoked in order to destroy the Home Rule movement but more particularly to derail the movement of the working class.

The UVF was a reactionary army comprising the most backward sections of the Protestant population. At the top it consisted entirely of aristocrats, businessmen, wealthy lawyers, church ministers, doctors, ex-army officers, etc. Lists of those who participated in its founding read like a Who's Who of the uppermost circles of society. As a special treat Sir George Richardson, an ex-officer in the British army, was called in to lead this force. His credentials were impeccable! His family history could boast distinguished service to imperialism. His grandfather fought for the East India Company, his father had played his part in the suppression of the Indian Mutiny. Following in father's footsteps, Sir George had joined the Indian army, had fought with Roberts in the Afghan campaign, and had really earned his credentials as a champion of "empire" when he had gone to China in 1900 to crush the Boxer Rebellion.

CHAPTER FOUR

Labour Unity & Reaction

A t the bottom the UVF mobilised the traditionally conservative elements among the rural Protestants, the petty bourgeoisie and the semi-demoralized lumpenproletariat of the towns. Some of its recruits were reported to have been those who attempted to scab on the workers of Belfast in 1907. Lenin compared this force to the reactionary Black Hundred gangs organised by the Tsar to persecute the forces of the revolution in Russia in the period after the defeat of the 1905 revolution. [19]

It is clear why such people have backed the loyalists. However, it is undoubtedly true that a broader section of the Protestant population, while not backing the military operations of the UVF, and while not participating in the mass rallies of Carson, did express an opposition to Home Rule. Among those, for example, who signed Carson's Covenant must be included sections of the Protestant workers. Socialists must be able to explain this situation.

Two major factors determined the attitude of the masses, particularly of the working class. The first was the character of the Home Rule movement and the second was the role which could be played by the labour movement.

The outburst of Orange sectarianism in 1911-14 was answered by an outburst of sectarianism, no less vile in its content, from nationalist politicians. After the demise and ultimately the death of Parnell the National League was splintered. The man who eventually emerged from the confusion as the new champion of nationalist Ireland was Redmond, a landlord in whom there existed not the slightest trace of sympathy for social agitation of any shape, size or form. It is said that one of the explanations for the purely halfhearted attempts of his party to extend the provisions of the 1903 Wyndham Land Act was the fact that Redmond personally stood to benefit greatly from the generous compensation terms it offered the landlords.

Part of the programme of the Redmondite nationalists for Ireland was the demand that under Home Rule the British government should not continue to pay welfare benefits to the Irish. This should be in the hands of the Irish

---

[19.] *Lumpenproletariat (a German word literally meaning "ragged proletariat") is a term that was originally coined by Karl Marx to describe sections of the working class which suffer from long-term unemployment and are unlikely to be connected with the trade union and labour movement.*

government. Effectively, with those of Redmond's outlook presenting themselves as the future form of government, this was a call for the exclusion from Irish soil of the embryo which then existed of a welfare state.

With the triumph of Redmondism the process of dividing the Irish struggle into separate strands of interests was complete. Nationalism stood aside and apart from the struggle of the Irish people to remove the yoke of economic oppression. Moving to the right under the circumstances developing at this period, they could not but move in the direction of sectarianism. By 1914 Redmond stood at the head of the Irish Volunteers. The Ancient Order of Hibernians and the United Irish League, both of which had gained strength as wings of the Irish Parliamentary Party after the death of Parnell. Each strove to outdo the other in sectarianism.

One section of the AOH which gained a basis of support in Belfast adorned itself with the title "Board of Erin". Primarily it was formed to protect Catholic small businessmen from the effects of racketeering in the city. In the end it became the instrument of the most vicious racketeering itself. One of the figures it could claim as a spokesman was "wee" Joe Devlin, later to emerge as a prime champion of the Catholic cause when the new Northern Ireland state was established after 1920. He was a man who, despite much flamboyant oratory to the contrary, played a part in ensuring that the cross of sectarianism remained tied to the backs of the working class. Devlin had shared platforms with that other "architect of nationalism" William Martin Murphy of 1913 fame. James Connolly summed up the Board of Erin when he described it as the "foulest brood which ever came into Ireland".[20]

Just as an illustration of the kind of fine sentiments being expressed by the Board of Erin leaders, it is worth quoting a few of the words of one of its representatives, a Professor Kettle, who, at a meeting in Wexford, announced, following disorders, "for such of the Orange Dogs as may have survived the riot... they should be shot or hanged or sent into penal servitude."

In opposition to the sectarianism of the right-wing nationalists there were a few moderates who, though no less conservative than the AOH breed, nevertheless recoiled from the blatant use of sectarianism. The leader of one such moderate splinter from the Parliamentary Party was William O'Brien. Of the sectarian Dillonite wing of the Nationalist Party he had this to say:

> "They transformed the National party and National movement into one from which not only all Unionists but all Protestants were excluded ... by subjecting the National movement to the new ascendancy of a sham Catholic secret society ..."

[20.] *The Ancient Order of Hibernians (AOH) is a right-wing, sectarian Catholic "fraternal" organisation set up as a Catholic equivalent to the Orange Order.*

In the end, rabid sectarianism won the day in such circles. Just as sections of the Protestant bourgeoisie who had been hesitant about the encouragement given to the Orange Order soon slipped into a minority, so too Green Toryism very quickly became Catholic Toryism and nothing more. Moving as it did to the right, avoiding the key social issues, it could not but have steered itself on such a sectarian course. In some cases this was a quite conscious move designed to break the unity of the working class. While Britain had invited, developed and deployed the art of "divide and rule", right-wing nationalists proved no amateurs at repeating this tactic.

In the 1900s as in the 1960s and 1970s both Green and Orange Tories had one thing in common — hatred of labour and socialism. Connolly found his ideas attacked by Catholic bigots and equally fiercely by Protestant bigots. In 1913, 400 aluminium workers in Larne joined the ITGWU. These men were working a seven-day week. In July they struck. Without a moment's hesitation the churches intervened. Ministers spent their time delivering lectures lamenting the "ease" with which these men were deceived by a popeish plot. Just as the Catholic children of Dublin were soon to be informed that starvation was preferable to risking their religion in Protestant homes, so the Protestant workers of Larne were now informed by their clerics that 84 hours' back-creaking toil was preferable to the sin of listening to "papishes".

On the opposite side the AOH devoted not a little of its propaganda to denouncing the evils of socialism and in particular attacking Connolly's Socialist Party of Ireland. Another organisation, founded in 1905, was Sinn Féin. This body likewise wasted no time in demonstrating that it took its stand with the Catholic businessmen, not with labour.

Its leader, Arthur Griffith, embodied in human frame both the aspirations and at the same time the weaknesses of large sections of the Southern Irish bourgeoisie. Griffith favoured tariff barriers behind which he dreamt that Irish capital could nurture itself. Like the bourgeoisie he had nothing to offer the struggle of the workers but venom. Rather he wished to see the English exploiters removed so that Irish exploiters would have a free hand in subjugating the population.

Sinn Féin published a newspaper, originally called the *United Irishman*, but re-titled *Sinn Féin* [21] in 1906. During the industrial battles of later years this journal denounced strikes, Larkinites, etc., and declared that strikes were an "English disease". Griffith himself favoured the establishment of an Irish monarchy — a mere swapping of tyrants!

Men like Griffith and Redmond symbolized the weakness of native Irish

---

[21.] *The United Irishman was an Irish nationalist newspaper co-founded by Arthur Griffith, the founder of Sinn Féin. It was first published on 4th March 1899 and ran until 1906. In 1906, the United Irishman collapsed under a libel suit and was refounded as Sinn Féin, which ran until 1914 when it was suppressed by the British government.*

capital. The small capitalist class who enjoyed an existence outside the Belfast area longed for an age when English capital would no longer dominate and curb their activities. Yet how could English capital be removed? Only by mobilizing the whole of society, including the workers and tenants. There lay the rub! For if the Southern capitalists resented English domination they were paralysed with fear of the Irish masses, and that fear counted a hundred times more in determining their role. Hence the Griffiths and the Redmonds, in the tradition of the Grattons, Floods, O'Connells and other middle-class and upper-class politicians, only led the national struggle in order to divert it away from the social issues so that some form or other of miserable compromise could be reached with imperialism. With wheeling and dealing they sought to dash the aspirations of their followers.

It takes no great mind whatsoever to understand why people of this ilk held no attraction whatsoever for the Protestant population of the North. With nationalism becoming synonymous with Catholicism and Green Toryism, even Protestant workers could be made to lean towards Unionism. As Connolly said in an article entitled Socialists and the Nation written as early as 1909,

"When a Sinn Féiner waxes eloquent about restoring the Constitution of '82, but remains silent about the increasing industrial despotism of the capitalist, when the Sinn Féiner speaks to men who are fighting against low wages and tells them that the Sinn Féin body has promised lots of Irish labour in Ireland, what wonder if they come to believe that a change from Toryism to Sinn Féin would simply change from the devil they know to the devil they do not know."

The hostility of the Protestant workers to the Home Rule movement was not the hostility of the Carsons, Craigs, etc. Both were class hostility and, coming from opposite ends of the social spectrum, both reflected totally different fears. The fear of the Orange bosses was of the Protestant and Catholic workers. The fear of the Protestant workers was of the self-interest of the aspiring Southern bourgeoisie and petty bourgeoisie.

Workers in Belfast inclined naturally to the industrial army in Liverpool, Glasgow and other major cities of Britain. In contrast, they looked to the rest of Ireland, and, with Dublin as the only major exception, they saw a largely agricultural country, with a nationalist leadership seeped in the reactionary mentality of the petty bourgeoisie. They saw from every corner the hostility of the nationalists to labour. What would happen to the unions, to the rights of labour, in an independent Ireland? These were the questions in the minds of the workers. Semi-conscious fears, they were given conscious expression by those who sought to sow the seeds of sectarian division.

Groups of trade unionists who supported the Union were organised by the Carsonites. In 1914 a group of Protestant trade unionists held a rally in the Ulster Hall to state their opposition to Home Rule. They attacked the Belfast Trades Council for its pro-Home Rule stance. A manifesto issued before the meeting attempted to explain their support for the anti-Home-Rule movement.

Its propaganda speaks volumes about the real attitudes of the workers. Learned treatises on the benefits of the Union from merchants, landowners and manufacturers could cut little ice. No exaltations about the link with UK capital could convince those who lived in the hovels and laboured in the workshops of industrial Belfast. Empty phrases about the "defence of the Protestant heritage and way of life" on their own could attract no mass support among the workers. To be effective, the propaganda of Unionism had to be translated into class terms. Thus this manifesto had to couch its arguments in such terms as:

> "The Irish people under the Home Rule Bill can pass labour laws for Ireland... under an Irish parliament controlled by small farmers, the Factory Acts would remain a dead letter". Also the following: "We know that the privilege won for the workers by trade unionism are in danger and that the loss of these privileges means the degradation of labour in Ireland, a result which sooner or later must do irreparable harm to the trade union movement in Britain."

Thus the enemies of the working class, including the agents of sectarianism within their own ranks, attempted to dupe and mislead the masses. Only one could have allayed the fears of the workers and put an end to sectarianism – the labour movement. The Irish bourgeoisie were themselves divided and were capable only of dividing. In Connolly's words, the struggle for freedom had become the struggle of the most subject class in society for freedom.

In the textbooks of the ruling class the issue at stake in this period was simply whether the Unionists could manage to destroy Home Rule or whether the nationalists would emerge with the prize of quasi-independence. In reality the question was whether the Irish working class, through the unions and labour organisations, would rise up quickly enough, and with the necessary leadership, to avert the disaster impending whichever section of the bosses got their way.

Only if the labour movement was in the forefront would the suspicions of the Protestant workers be removed. Only if there was a struggle for more than a mere change of flag or parliament could the working people be united and mobilised. It would have to be a fight for the ownership of industry, the ownership of land, the ownership of capital. Rather than weakening itself by steering away from these social questions, its very strength would derive from them. Nor would it be a fight for mere independence. By slicing the rope tying the Irish people to English capital, the workers of Ireland would be forging a chain firmly linking themselves to the movement of the British and the international working classes.

Recognizing this, Connolly spent the years up until 1914 to build the labour movement and push it to the forefront. His activities gave expression to the aspirations of the advanced sections of the working class throughout Ireland. He was not prepared to see labour sit back while rival property interests fought over the future of "the nation", using working people as cannon fodder. Connolly recognized then, in an infinitely more difficult period for the young and barely tested workers' movement, what many of his so-called followers today have miserably failed to understand – that all-class alliances are recipes for sectarian division among the working class.

His prime concern, at this time, was not to concoct unholy alliances with petty-bourgeois nationalists but rather to ensure that the struggle against British rule would be indelibly stamped with the demands of the workers' organisations for workers' rule.

His position was for independent action by all sections of the labour movement. When the nationalist Volunteers were beginning their campaign of armed marches, Connolly recognized the need for the workers organisations to keep their distance from such groups. After 1913, sections of the Citizen Army, including individuals at its head such as Captain White, argued for the merging of this body with the Irish Volunteers. Connolly fought all such efforts and succeeded in maintaining the tiny Citizen Army as the special armed wing of the trade union movement, guarding for example the premises of the ITGWU in Dublin. [22]

Symptomatic of Connolly's attitude was his attempt to crush sectarianism in the North. Faced with sectarian emblems, parades, bands, etc., he did not, unlike the Labour leaders of the 1960s and 1970s, throw up his hands in despair, wax eloquent about "tribal warfare", and then permit the movement to roll over on its back and play dead. Rather he seized every opportunity for action.

The prominence of the Home Rule issue was used by the bosses to sow division among the workers. Thus, in 1912, the true target of the Carsonites and their fellows was shown to be the unity of the working class. Using an at-

---

[22.] *The Irish Citizen Army (ICA) was a small armed group of workers established in Dublin for the defence of workers' demonstrations from the Dublin Metropolitan Police during the 1913 lockout.*

tack by AOH members on a Sunday school parade as a pretext, the bosses in the North incited sectarian attacks during the 12th of July celebrations of that year. As a result workers were expelled from the shipyards and from other industries. Socialists and Catholics, in that order, were the targets. Connolly reacted to this and other violence by organizing labour demonstrations. He even formed a non-sectarian Labour Band for the purpose. His answer to the July troubles was to march with labour banners and labour music through the centre of Belfast. It was intended as a physical expression of workers' unity and of independent action by the labour organisations.

In 1913 Connolly stood as Labour candidate in the Dock ward in Belfast. Again, this bold determination to raise and push to the forefront the idea of labour unity articulated the urgent need felt by the most advanced sections of the working class for action in defiance of the sectarians. Reflecting this is the fact that Belfast Trades Council gave its official support to Connolly's candidature. During this campaign Connolly was attacked by bigots on both sides, notable the AOH. In the end he polled 905 votes against 1523 won by the Unionist.

Similarly in 1914 Connolly pressed the ITUC to move on to the political sphere in order that the voice of labour could be more clearly heard throughout Ireland. Also at the 1914 Congress of the ITUC a motion condemning partition, again moved by Connolly, was passed, with only two delegates out of the 94 present voting against on the grounds that the motion was "political", not on the grounds of supporting the carving of Ireland in two.

When Redmond and Devlin appeared to be prepared to accept such a compromise as the "temporary" partition of the country, Connolly warned that this "would perpetrate in a form, aggravated in evil, the discords now prevalent, and help the Home Rule and Orange capitalists and clerics to keep their rallying cries before the public as the political watchwords of the day". In 1914 he urged intensive action on the part of labour to offset such an evil:

"Such a scheme as that agreed to by Redmond and Devlin, the betrayal of the nationalist democracy of Industrial Ulster, would set back the wheels of progress, would destroy the oncoming unity of the Irish labour movement and paralyse all advanced movements whilst it endured. To it Labour should give the bitterest opposition, against it Labour should fight even to the death, if necessary, like our forefathers before us."

The question whether the young labour movement could develop quickly enough to avert the catastrophe of any form of bosses' solution to the Irish problem was not answered in this period. Before 1914 this movement was squaring up to the realities of class war on a scale never before witnessed in Ireland. The young proletariat revealed its strength and determination in these battles. It had a major asset in the revolutionary leadership beginning to develop in the form of Connolly and Larkin. But the movement was still young. Its political voice was not yet decisively raised. It had engaged in years of bitter and exhausting struggle and had emerged neither victorious nor routed. The task of Connolly and other socialists was made immense by these factors. To push to the foreground of the consciousness of the entire proletariat of Ireland the question of labour unity, to thwart the armed movement of the national struggle out of the hands of the right-wing nationalists and into the hands of workers' organisations – these were no small objectives.

War, four years of indescribable carnage in pursuit of economic domination, cut across both the development of labour, and also the rise of the Unionist and nationalist armies. Whether labour could place itself at the head of the national struggle in time to avert whatever disaster would be imposed by the Redmonites, Carsonites or the British government – this question was postponed, not answered.

CHAPTER FIVE

Socialism or Division: 1914–1921

With the outbreak of war the various sections of the bourgeoisie agreed to put aside their differences and concentrate on the task at hand – the pouring of as much human raw material as possible into the trenches. In parliament the Liberals, the loyalists and even the nationalists vied with each other to show that they "put the nation first". Carson volunteered the postponement of the Home Rule debate until after the war. So did Redmond. So too did Asquith.

The Irish problem had simplified itself as far as the bosses were concerned. It was now a problem of how to press-gang as many Irishmen as possible into uniform to go and serve their "King and Country" in Flanders. Conscription was favoured by many sections of the ruling class. However, a number of factors had prevented its implementation. First there was the question of opinion in America. The prime concern of the British bosses was to bring America into the war – on their side. The American government, with all its superficial phrasemongering about defending the rights of small nations, would have to be sensitive to the tide of pro-Irish feeling at home. It would have had difficulty justifying an ally which practised its defence of the rights of small nations by coercing unwilling Irishmen into its army. Secondly the very problem of implementing the policy of conscription without tying down huge numbers of troops in Ireland to maintain order was a deterrent. Finally, and particularly towards the end of the war, of major importance was opposition to conscription from the ranks of an aroused Irish labour movement.

If the Irish could not be press-ganged into uniform, more gentle measures would have to be employed! And what better than to employ the trusted leaders of the nationalist movement to plead the case of imperialism to the Irish people?

By 1914 Redmond proved most patriotic! Not only did he support the war;

he even offered to use the Volunteers to look after security in Ireland so that the British garrison would be free for use in Europe. Of course the British preferred that the Irish Volunteers serve in the trenches so that their troops could be spared to keep order in Ireland.

And Redmond willingly obliged! He expended not a little energy touring the country to address recruiting meetings. With him were the other leaders of right-wing nationalism. As Connolly pointed out, the self-same people who denounced the workers of Dublin in 1913 for sending children to "Protestant" homes to avoid starvation were now, with gusto, encouraging the youth of Ireland to clamber into khaki uniforms and shed their blood in the interests of their masters. In Dublin one of the slogans of the recruiting meetings was that the "trenches are safer than the slums". Because of the risk of disease in the miserable hovels of Dublin's ghettos this may well have been the case. Never more clearly had capitalism been indicted by the people who spent their time trying to preserve it than it had through this slogan.

Redmond was highly successful during the early war years in his recruiting efforts. The initial wave of jingoism which had accompanied the war had even stretched itself into Ireland. It had combined with the miseries of life in the slums and on the land, to drive some 200,000 Irish people into the army.

Those who volunteered, thanks to the efforts of the nationalists, found themselves scattered throughout the regiments of the British army. A concentration of Irish soldiers in any regiment would have spelt danger to the control which could be exercised by the army chiefs. These reactionaries who made up the bulk of Carson's UVF received different treatment. The special 36th (Ulster) Division was formed almost entirely from the ranks of the UVF.

The overwhelming majority of the National Volunteers backed Redmond's stance in 1914. When a few more militant sections of the Volunteers such as the secret Irish Republican Brotherhood talked in terms of "England's difficulty" being "Ireland's opportunity", they were largely scorned or ignored.

CHAPTER SIX

Connolly and 1916

Among the few people who stood out against the war was James Connolly. In 1914 he was one of a handful of socialists internationally who denounced the carnage as an imperialist war. He stood with Lenin, Trotsky, Liebknecht, Luxemburg, and a few others, in his denunciations.[23]

In pitiful contrast were the leaders of the major social-democratic parties and major unions in Europe. These gentlemen had met in 1912 at the Basle Congress and resolved that the outbreak of war would be answered by an international general strike which would paralyse the war effort of every country. When the armies of Europe eventually descended upon each other, tossing worker against worker, the initial outburst of national chauvinism which accompanied the first shots was sufficient to dissolve the opposition of almost all the leaders of European social democracy. Inevitably those at the top of the strongest movements, with the greatest power at their disposal, became the most rotten, the most cowardly and the most open in their support of the war effort.

Faced with, and outraged by, these betrayals, Connolly, more than any other leader in Ireland, was determined that action on the part of the Irish people was necessary. He pressed the leaders of the IRB and the Volunteers to organise an insurrection. Suspicious of the role of the leaders of these organisations, he even threatened that if they were not prepared to rise he would do so, using only the tiny forces of the Citizen Army. On one occasion, he told his son that he thought the Volunteer leaders were prepared to fight only if they had "steam-heated trenches".

When plans for a rising during Easter week 1916 were agreed, Connolly's reservations about the role of the nationalist leaders were shown to be well founded. Connolly had once described the nationalist leaders as "the open enemies or the treacherous friends of the working class". McNeill, the commander of the Volunteers, on the day before the 1916 rising, actually sent out an order stating that it had been called off. Arthur Griffith expressed vehement opposition to this "lunacy" and split away from all the

---

[23] *This refers to Vladimir Lenin and Leon Trotsky, leaders of the Russian Revolution, and also Karl Liebknecht and Rosa Luxemburg, who were murdered by far-right forces during the German revolution in January 1919*

groups that were involved. During the actual fighting he had a "change of heart" and offered support but was told by the insurgents to stand aside and instead concentrate on political back-up work. His subsequent arrest proved fortunate for his political career, since, in the minds of the people, if not in actual fact, it placed him side by side with the "heroes" of 1916.

On the morning of Easter Monday 1916 little more than a thousand men marched to the GPO in the centre of Dublin. There the flag of independence was raised and a proclamation read. Other buildings throughout the city were seized, including the Four Courts, the South Dublin Union and Bolands Mill. The reaction of the military establishment was swift. Despite Connolly's prediction, probably given to reassure his somewhat unwilling troops, that the capitalists would not shell their own property, within one day, artillery was being used against the insurgents.

Outside Dublin only a few areas were affected. In Galway over a thousand men were mobilised by Liam Mellows, only to be dispersed after several skirmishes. The town of Enniscorthy in Wexford was held for a time. Elsewhere there was little activity, except in North County Dublin, where a railway line was seized.

After one week of fighting, the Dublin rising was bloodily suppressed. Lacking any real basis of support, the insurgents did not have the slightest chance of victory. In fact, as the captured men were marched through the streets of Dublin in many cases they were met with the derision and abuse of the people. In Dame Street, a crowd actually waved Union Jacks in their faces. Elsewhere, in Thomas Street, for example, tomatoes and other fruit were hurled at them.

There followed a programme of executions. General Maxwell, the head of the British forces, demanded that a grim example be made of the insurgents. Ninety people were sentenced to be executed by firing squad. As the programme of executions got under way, demands for clemency grew in both Britain and Ireland. But the executions continued – continued, that is, until Connolly was dead. Then, with the greatest leader of the workers in Ireland dead, the killings were ended. Not surprisingly the Irish Independent, owned by William Martin Murphy, that money-grabbing capitalist of 1913, raised the call for clemency only after one of his arch-enemies, Connolly, had been shot.

Murphy's stance was indicative of that of the entire establishment and business community in Ireland. When such representatives of Irish capitalism as millionaire Charles Haughey and others pay lip service to the "national heroes" of 1916 they deserve to be reminded that their class took a somewhat different position at the time of the rising. To a man, the capitalists of Ireland made themselves hoarse in 1916 by shouting their denunciations of Connolly, Pearse and Co.

The Irish Times in an editorial at the time celebrated the fact that "Liberty Hall is no more than a sinister and hateful memory." On May 8 it insisted that the execution of leaders should continue. Calling for military rule to be extended, it stated:

> "We have learned that the sword of the soldier is a far better guarantee of justice and liberty than the presence of the politician."

Alongside Murphy, the Dublin Chamber of Commerce opposed the rising. So did the church. So did the ragbag of right-wing sectarian organisations such as the Ancient Order of Hibernians and the Irish National Foresters. "Respectable Dublin", the kith and kin of the present rulers of Southern Ireland were not in the GPO during Easter week 1916. From their drawing rooms and parlors they were praising and encouraging the British forces. In their speeches and publications they were wholeheartedly demanding retribution in full against those who dared physically to oppose the national oppression of Ireland.

Few incidents in Irish history have been subject to such confusion and distortion as the 1916 rising. In particular, the participation of Connolly, fighting with the people he did, under the Irish flag, and as signatory to a declaration which demanded that the Irish people, not the Irish working class, should be the owners of Ireland, has sown endless confusion. Connolly's role in 1916 has been and still is used by countless petty-bourgeois nationalists, republicans, "Green" so-called socialists and a hundred and one other self-ordained "followers" to give license to the crimes which they commit against the working class movement in his name.

Connolly stands as a giant when compared to all the other leaders, apart from Larkin, who have dominated the Irish labour movement before 1916 or since. His contribution in terms of ideas has not been surpassed. His readiness to struggle at all times and to make endless sacrifice has not been matched. In 1916 his motive was the advancement of the interests of the class he had faithfully served throughout his life as a conscious socialist.

Neither before nor during the 1916 rising did Connolly have any illusions in his nationalist "allies". On the eve of the fighting he addressed the Citizen Army with the following words:

"the odds against are 1000-1. But if we should win, hold onto your rifles, because the Volunteers may have a different goal. Remember we are out not only for political liberty but for economic liberty as well. So hold onto your rifles."

Albeit with the very best motives, Connolly was nevertheless mistaken in 1916 in concocting the type of alliance he did between himself and the nationalists, and in doing this on the terms that he did. There were occasions in the pre-rising period when he even spoke on platforms with such right-wing petty-bourgeois enemies of the working class as Arthur Griffith. His decision in 1916 to fly the green flag over Dublin's GPO, rather than have the Citizen Army march and fight separately under the red flag, was a decision which was not supported by many of his followers within the Citizen Army even at that time. But this mistake was not made because Connolly had a change of heart about the very people whom he had viciously polemicised against before the war.

Nor was Connolly at any time motivated by mere narrow, nationalist sentiments. His "mistake" in 1916 was made for the best of reasons. The battle of Dublin workers in 1913 had temporarily exhausted the movement of the Irish working class. During the war there were strikes, some successful, but never did the movement even begin to rise to the crescendo of the struggles of the pre-war period. The betrayal of the great lockout by the leaders of the British trade unions, and the mood of exhaustion which swept the Irish labour movement thereafter, undoubtedly had an effect on Connolly himself. His partial disorientation caused by these events was confounded by the outbreak of the war.

After 1914 his prime concern was with the war and the mood of jingoism which swept sections of the population. Aghast at the gross betrayal perpetrated by the tops of the workers' movement internationally in 1914, and shocked that the carnage could rage for two years without any opposition, he looked in desperation for some way of provoking a movement against the war. He was prepared to sacrifice himself, his organisation, and even to compromise on some of his ideas, in order to set the workers' movement once again on a forward path. This attitude of struggle stands in marked contrast to the cringing chauvinism of the social-democratic leaders internationally who discarded their socialism in favour of patriotic phrases throughout this period. Connolly was isolated in his denunciation of the war. He could not see even a ripple of a class movement in Europe and therefore he decided to use every possible means and every possible ally, to create such opposition in Ireland:

"Should the working class of Europe rather than slaughter each other for the benefit of the King and financiers proceed tomorrow to erect barricades all over Europe, to break up bridges and destroy transport services that war might be abolished, we should be perfectly happy in following such a glorious example and contributing our aid to the final dethronement of the vulture class that rule and rob the world. But pending either of these consummations it is our manifest duty to take all possible action to save the poor from the horrors this war has in store."

A revolutionary duty, not just to fight against national domination in Ireland, but to the international struggle against class domination – this was Connolly's view of the need for a rising. As he graphically put it, the hope was that a rising would "set the torch to a European conflagration that will not burn out until that last capitalist bond and debenture will be shrivelled on the funeral pyre of the last warlord."

The mistake of the Easter rising was not so much that it took place, but that it took place prematurely. Connolly was wrong when he argued that it would ignite the class movement in Europe. The theory that any group of workers can be detonated into action by heroic example is false. Only when the conditions for mass struggle actually exist, only when the masses are prepared to do battle and make enormous sacrifices, can a mass revolutionary movement be created. Many of those who advocate the false tactics of individual guerrilla warfare today draw, in part, their inspiration from the Easter rising. If they removed their blindfolds they would discover that the actual experience of the rising proved the futility of isolated action.

In any case the 1916 rising was an attempted insurrection, not a part of a guerrilla campaign. Had Connolly had the slightest illusion in the methods of individual terror, he had ample scope to use such methods between 1914 and 1916. Not only did he have the "opportunity" provided by the war, he had an armed organisation in the Citizen Army. But Connolly during these years neither conducted, nor advocated a campaign of bombings and shootings.

The conditions for mass revolutionary action expressly did not exist in 1916. They did not exist in Ireland and they did not exist in Europe. In Ireland, the IRB and the Citizen Army were only a handful in number.

True, the advanced workers had stood out against the war. All the groups who fought in 1916 were working-class in composition. The Citizen Army was the army of the workers led by workers' leaders. The other organisations, such as the IRB, while their leadership was petty bourgeois, were chiefly made up of workers, albeit largely of white-collar workers. In fact many of the Volunteers

were people who had wished to join the Citizen Army but who had been refused because of lack of equipment. Yet these advanced sections of the class
had not gathered behind them the active support of the mass the workers and
the small farmers and farm labourers.

In the period after the industrial battles of 1913, and because of the jingoism
which had accompanied the war, Connolly had actually on some occasions advised against strikes because of the depleted resources of the ITGWU. Activity
within the workers' organisations remained low-key right up until 1916.

A reflection of this, and also of Connolly's desperation to stage an insurrection, no matter how hopeless, was the lack of any real preparation for a rising. The power of several thousand armed men is one thing. Such power, linked
to the overwhelming might of organised labour, is something entirely different.
A general strike to paralyze supplies and to bring the masses into activity was
an ABC demand. Yet even Connolly did not raise it.

Even within the Citizen Army and among the labour activists, opposition
to the war had not yet crystallized to the extent of broad support for an uprising.
Connolly used his tremendous authority as a revolutionary leader, and a trade
union organiser, to drag his men behind him. He ignored criticism from the
other leaders of the Irish Transport and General Workers' Union because his
sights were set on action, no matter how futile.

It is an incredible fact that at the Congress of the Irish Trade Unions and
Labour Party which met in August 1916 no separate protest was made about
the execution of Connolly. Instead the Congress leaders tried to be all things to
all people by proposing a minute silence to both the dead of the Easter rising
and those killed in the trenches of Europe. This, despite the fact that Connolly
had, prior to 1916, been, in Larkin's absence, acting general secretary of the
ITGWU. Many of his opponents within the trade union movement would not
have been disheartened to see him removed from activity within the unions.
But the fact that no protest occurred reflected not only the opportunism of the
Congress leadership but also the lack of any mass basis of active support among
the trade union rank and file for Connolly's participation in the rising.

The difference between Connolly and other Marxists such as Lenin and
Trotsky was that they maintained a perspective for future struggles and were
thus capable of preserving their ideas despite the most difficult objective circumstances. Lenin understood that events would turn themselves inside out.
He saw that the same war which had reduced the revolutionary wing of social
democracy to a handful in 1914 would itself be a generating factor in producing
a new wave of class storms which would shake Europe.

In 1916 the tiny forces of those internationalists who stood out against the war attended a conference at Zimmerwald in Switzerland. It was joked that the entire forces of international revolution at that time could be put into the few coaches which carried them to the conference. And of those attending only a minority were prepared to give support to the ideas of Lenin and the Bolsheviks. Yet this tiny, tiny nucleus, because it applied the tested methods of Marxism, was able, on the basis of a movement of the masses themselves, to become the centre of the new and mass revolutionary organisation of the international working class.

In Dublin, in 1916 it was the advanced workers in the main who fought. Thus the flower of the Irish proletariat rose up, but was slaughtered, before the movement really began in Europe. The tragedy of the rising lies in this fact. Above all the most farsighted leader of the Irish workers, the most outstanding Marxist to have emerged from the British or Irish labour movement, was dead. No Marxist party had been created by Connolly to carry on his struggle and keep alive his real ideas and his real traditions. A large section of the head and of the brain of the workers' movement was destroyed – and was destroyed before the really decisive movement of the class as a whole had begun. Into the vacuum stepped a whole breed of shabby opportunists ready to lavish praise on men like Connolly, in order to trample on the traditions of revolutionary struggle which, throughout his whole life, Connolly had maintained.

Alongside the fact that the action was premature, Connolly was also incorrect in the manner in which he participated in the rising. He should have fought on his own programme, not on the vague ideas contained in the proclamation read from the steps of Dublin's GPO on the first day. Much of the present day confusion surrounding Connolly's role would never have arisen had he clearly presented his own alternative programme. Had he issued a call to the workers of Ireland and of the world on the question of hours of work, of wages, of factory conditions, and of the ownership of the land, the banks and the major industries by the working class, his clear socialist ideas would not have been open to the slightest misinterpretation.

Connolly had given up none of these objectives in 1916. He ensured, for example, during the rising, that the flag of Irish labour, the Starry Plough, was raised above the Imperial Hotel, owned by Martin Murphy. But in his efforts to ensure that a rising went ahead he had been prepared to compromise on ideas with members of the IRB. That mistake has opened up a chink in the armour of Connolly's socialist thought and has allowed people who are opposed to everything for which Connolly sacrificed his entire existence to pretend to stand in his shoes.

Of course, all the mistakes which Connolly was prepared to make in order to prepare for the rising, his alliance with the nationalists, his willingness to temporarily forgo aspects of the socialist programme, have been exalted to positions of "genius" and "examples to be followed". His real contempt for the petty-bourgeois nature of the nationalist movement, his uncompromising revolutionary ideas, the real reasons why he pushed for an insurrection, have too often been forgotten. Coalitions, dirty deals of all sorts with all types of people who, were he alive today, would have fought tooth and nail against Connolly are prepared to toast his memory. As Connolly himself once commented, "apostles of freedom are ever idolized when dead but crucified when living".

Those who justify coalitions between the workers' organisations and other political parties on the basis of Connolly's participation in the 1916 rising would do well to study Connolly's whole lifetime experience of struggle against such unholy alliances. On January 22, 1916 he made a statement which many leaders of the labour movement would do well to digest today: "The labour movement is like no other movement. Its strength lies in being like no other movement. It is never so strong as when it stands alone." At the turn of the century the French socialist leader, Millerand, accepted a position in the French cabinet. Connolly denounced this betrayal, on the basis that a workers' party should "accept no government position which it cannot conquer through its own strength at the ballot box". He denounced Millerand's stand by saying that "what good Millerand may have done is claimed for the credit of the bourgeois republican government: what evil the cabinet has done reflects back on the reputation of the socialist parties. Heads they win, tails we lose." It takes no genius to work out what stand Connolly would have taken on the Southern coalition between the organisation that he helped to create, the Irish Labour Party, and the group of former blueshirts who call themselves Fine Gael.

In 1917 the perspectives of Lenin and Trotsky were borne out by the events in Russia. In February of that year the workers of Russia rose up and swept aside tsarism. Only because the political consciousness of this movement, and of its leadership, was still at a low level, this did not immediately result in the passing of power into the hands of the workers, but in the emergence of a Constituent Assembly including representatives of the capitalist parties. However, side by side with this body, the workers established their own organisations – the soviets or workers' councils.

It was soon apparent that the programme of piecemeal reform could not ease the burden of the Russian workers and peasants and could not put an end to the war. The soldiers and workers were demanding peace and bread. The peasants were demanding the land. The liberal capitalists could provide none of these. And so the task of implementing these demands fell to the working class, who also carried out their programme, the abolition of capitalist rule. In October 1917 the Bolshevik Party, supported by the mass of the population, wrested power from the bosses and established the most democratic form of government which has ever existed – rule by the soviets.

Thus were vividly demonstrated the importance of clear ideas, correct tactics and above all a perspective of future events. Before October 1917 the Bolsheviks had warned against premature attempts to seize power. In July the workers in the cities, en masse, had been champing at the bit. But the Bolsheviks urged caution, advising that the mood in the countryside and army was not yet at a revolutionary pitch. The workers, provoked by the government, refused to sit back, and the July demonstrations were suppressed by the government. Because the Bolsheviks, despite their advice to the workers not to go onto the streets with arms at that stage, did not turn their backs on those workers who did demonstrate, but put themselves at the head of the demonstrations, the movement was able to retreat in good order. By October 1917 the revolutionary fever had infected the countryside. The soldiers were ready to turn their backs on the trenches and to face their officers. Genuine mass support for the seizure of power existed. The Bolsheviks were able to carry through a successful insurrection. As a result of this overwhelming support Petrograd was in the hands of the workers with the loss of only ten lives. Moscow, the second city, fell within a week. What a sharp contrast with the bitter experience of the Dublin workers! After a week of fighting in which over 1300 people were killed or wounded, defeat was the result. A tradition of struggle had been maintained – but at a terrible cost to the working-class movement.

CHAPTER SEVEN

Working-Class Offensive

Easter week 1916 did not set the spark for the European conflagration hoped for by Connolly. The Russian revolution did. Here again is underlined the importance of correct perspectives, and of the ability to evaluate precisely the mood of the masses. With the Russian workers in power the international situation was transformed. Despite the crude distortions later laid upon these events by the Stalinist bureaucracy which was later to emerge and usurp the democratic institutions and traditions of the Soviet state including the soviets themselves, Lenin and Trotsky never conceived of socialism being built in Russia alone. Internationalists to the core, the Bolsheviks saw the Russian revolution as part and parcel of the international socialist revolution.

1917 produced an enormous revolutionary wave which swept across Europe. Revolutionary situations developed in Hungary, Italy and France. In Germany in 1918 workers returned from the front lines to find they had sacrificed themselves for a future of destitution at home. Towards the end of that year a series of upheavals actually left the working class in virtual control of the country. Whole towns and cities were for a time in the hands of the German workers' organisations. A piece of thread would have been strong enough to tie the hands of German capitalism at that stage. All that was needed was the final half-step to the consolidation of workers' rule. Then the bells would really have begun to toll not only for German but for world capitalism. That half-step forward was not taken. No Lenin, no Bolshevik party sufficiently strong, existed in that country. Instead, the utterly rotten leadership of the German social democracy, by leaving the machinery of the state and the wealth of the country in the grip of the capitalists, took several paces backwards.

These revolutionary developments, mirroring discontent nurtured by the war itself, rekindled the class struggles which had been cut across in 1914.

In many countries the pace of class warfare had been accelerating before

1914. War had cut across and actually reversed this process. But the war also laid down the conditions for a resumption of the struggle, at an even faster pace and with even more dire consequences for the bosses.

In Ireland, as elsewhere, this was the case. Between 1918 and 1921 the class movement which had developed was the major preoccupation of all sections of society. It transformed the national movement. It convulsed the labour movement, North and South. It determined the attitude of the bosses in Britain. It struck dread into the hearts of the reactionary Unionists and right-wing nationalists alike.

It is impossible in a brief space to give an impression of the extent of the movement. All that can be given is a catalogue of only a few of the major developments so that readers may draw their own conclusions.

Moves to impose conscription in 1918 were answered by a general strike. Over 1,500 delegates from the shop floor and from union branches came to Dublin in 1918 to discuss the organisation of this strike. They returned to their areas and on April 23 were successful in closing shops and factories throughout the country, except in Belfast. This movement was enough to persuade the government to hold its hand on this issue.

After 1918 the struggle in the South took a different turn as the opening shots of the War of Independence were fired. However, although many labour leaders and nationalist leaders willed otherwise, the class struggle would not wait. In 1920-21 the southwest of the country became the centre of a series of major battles which showed how far the workers were prepared to go in their demands.

County Clare was convulsed with land seizures. Soviets were actually established in rural areas in this relatively backward and isolated part of the country. In 1920 workers in the Knocklong Creamery took over the enterprise and ran it as a cooperative. Their slogan was "We make butter, not profits". The following year the workers in the Arigna coalmines in County Leitrim seized the mines and raised the red flag above their pits. Above all, the workers of Limerick demonstrated the mood of the working class as a whole when in 1919 they took over and ran the entire city as a soviet. They even printed their own money and controlled the prices of all goods within Limerick during this period.

At the top of the movement the leaders mouthed revolutionary phrases but made no attempt to swing the might of the industrial workforce of the east of the country behind these takeovers in the west. The full potential was not tapped. Yet what would have been possible was unmistakably shown.

In 1920 political prisoners in Mountjoy jail arrested under the "Defence of the Realm" regulations went on hunger strike. The working class, which, other than on this occasion, had been held apart from the national struggle, intervened and intervened decisively. A general strike was called in support of the prisoners. Industry was closed throughout the country outside Belfast. As in 1918 during the strike against conscription, shopkeepers and other middle layers of society backed the workers. On the second day of the strike against conscription, shopkeepers and other middle layers of society decisively backed the workers. On the second day of the strike the government recognized the "injustice" of imprisoning these men! In other words, they recognized the power of the working class and the dangerous consequences if that power were to weld itself behind the struggle for full independence. Such a dire consideration forced a change of heart. All prisoners concerned were released.

There were other, not less "dangerous" incidents when the workers' organisations, despite the timidity of their leaders, involved themselves in the fight against oppression. For example, in 1920 the Dublin dockers refused to unload munitions from Britain. In May of that year railway workers refused to transport soldiers.

A further indication of the rising pulse of class activity was the situation within the unions themselves. From the position of 1916 when the ITGWU had been reduced to a paltry 5,000 members, and possessed recorded assets of as little as £96, by 1921 that union could boast over 130,000 members.

All this represents a movement of revolutionary proportions. Such a movement knows no boundaries and scorns artificial barriers. It is profoundly and truly inspirational in scope. In Ireland the struggle did not develop in the North separately from the South or vice versa. Precisely the same infectious tide of militancy as gripped the South after 1918 also gripped the industrial area of the North by the throat.

1919 opened a general struggle for shorter hours in Britain and Ireland. In February 1919 a special Union and Labour Congress in Ireland issued a call for a 150 percent wage rise and a 44-hour week. This congress undoubtedly took its cue from the magnificent struggle of the Belfast engineering workers which had begun in January. These workers had come out behind the demand for a reduction in their basic hours from 54 to 44.

A TUC deal offered a reduction to 47 hours. The workers reacted against this "betrayal". First of all in Belfast the demand for 44 hours became the focus for mass action. Then in Glasgow and other parts of Britain similar movements erupted, in some places with the demand for 40 hours being raised.

The Belfast strike began with a magnificent display of mass solidarity. On 14th January, 1919, 20,000 shipyard and engineering workers downed tools and marched to the City Hall to a mass meeting, from which they went to their union halls to vote on the TUC deal of 47 hours. A little over a thousand workers voted in favor of the deal, while over 20,000 both rejected it and voted for strike action to achieve their own ends. At noon on January 25 the strike itself was begun.

After one week of strike action 40,000 workers were out and a further 20,000 were laid off. Almost every day there were mass meetings in various parts of the city. There was mass picketing of several factories. For almost four weeks the working class were in virtual control of the city. Transport, electricity, gas, most public services, the major engineering firms and the shipyards were all involved. Clerical as well as manual employees of Belfast Corporation had been brought out.

These four weeks provide a never-to-be-forgotten demonstration of the power of the working class. In Belfast the workers became the government. They controlled what moved and determined what did not move. At the center of this power were the recognized organisations of the working class, the strike committee itself and also the Belfast Trades Council. During the dispute the strike committee published its own newspaper which kept the workers informed of the strike activities.

As with trades councils in many British cities during the 1926 general strike, the Belfast Trades Council in 1919 according to its official history became a virtual organ of workers' government in the city. As this history records the event:

"To an increasing extent the Belfast Trades Council was looked towards as the leadership of the people. The Council formed itself into a 'Council of Action' and to a great extent had control over the movement of goods in the city."

Reaction was held at bay by the power of the workers. Initial attempts to invoke sectarianism only added to the workers' strength. At the beginning of February the Orange Order had hung out its true colours by publishing a manifesto calling for a return to work. This document also chose to comment on the strike leaders – pointing out that leaders of the Labour Party were involved. The capitalist press foamed at the mouth at the activities of the strikers. Each issue of the Belfast Newsletter lamented the manner in which the "Bolsheviks and Sinn Féiners" could mislead the "good workmen" of Belfast.

Such shrieks of horror failed absolutely to dent the solidarity of the strike.

Religious division was demolished by this strike movement. Symbolic of this was the composition of the strike committee itself. The majority of its members were Protestant, but the chairman was a Catholic. As in 1907, and to an even greater extent, it was demonstrated as an absolute law of history that, when the workers' movement goes forward, sectarianism, together with all the other backward tendencies in society, is forced to retreat. Only vacillation, backsliding or defeat, on the part of organised labour, gives these reactionary tendencies the opportunity to regain a foothold.

A concrete example of the way in which the labour movement can deal with the menace of sectarianism was given. At the beginning of the dispute a few sectarian and hooligan incidents did occur. There was some looting in the city centre. The workers reacted quickly. A body of about 2,000 men was set up to patrol the city, and keep it free of intimidation, looting, etc. For a brief moment in history the working class managed to suspend in mid-air the state machine of the exploiters and impose workers' law and workers' order.

Sir Richard Dawson Bates, who had been secretary to the UUC, and who was to be rewarded for his services by an appointment as Northern Ireland's first Minister for Home Affairs in 1921, wrote to Sir James Craig about the strike. In his letter he revealed, for all who care to see, the total impotence of the forces of the state and the Unionist leaders when confronted with the might of the organised working class. The question of the use of troops, he reveals, was discussed and dismissed as "inadvisable".

"I had several talks with Hacket-Pain who, notwithstanding a certain amount of pressure from scaremongers, declined to bring out troops, or do anything to make the workers think that they were being intimidated. What one wants to try to get the workers to see is that no one is really against them, except themselves: that the question is not a local one but a national one." In other words the use of troops might have had the dangerous consequence of driving together the workers North and South and utterly destroying the credibility of the Unionists.

Bates also reveals that, desperately wanting to put an end to the strike, the Unionists thought of intervening. He advises against by outlining the consequences of such an action: "I am firmly convinced that at the present time it would be most injudicious to drag Carson or any of the other leaders into it. In the first place they were not consulted as to going out on strike, and in the second place, if the men went back unsatisfied they would subsequently say that they were 'let down' by their unionist political leaders". "However," his advice continues: "If the workers indicate a desire to go back, pending a national arrangement being carried out, the question of getting the political leaders over to mediate is a question that could subsequently be raised." Thus, panic-stricken at the thought that intervention on their part would propel the workers into political opposition to Unionism, but on the other hand driven on by their class interests, the Unionists hovered like vultures waiting for a first sign of the weakness of their enemy before intervening.

Initially direct intervention by bigots and by the state was restrained. The bosses trembled at the possibility of provoking an even fiercer movement of workers. Instead they waited for the first signs that the momentum was waning. The first setback for the strike came from its own leaders. By the end of the second week it was clear that extra force would need to be applied to pressure the bosses to concede their demands. The support had been promised by transport workers, dockers and railwaymen. But the strike committee hesitated and drew back from involving these sections. Thus the total power of the working class was not fully realized.

February 12th brought a major setback. Faced with police batons and ultimately with troops, machine-gun emplacements and even tanks, the workers of Glasgow admitted defeat. From this moment the Belfast workers were isolated. Discussions of settlement terms threatened to split them. A ballot taken two days after the Glasgow defeat produced a majority of over 3,000 against settlement. But it revealed a sizeable minority of almost 9,000 prepared to return to work. It was a signal for the bosses to act.

That weekend, troops in battle gear occupied the gasworks and power stations. The Defence of the Realm Act was invoked to arrest two shop stewards who refused to work. Police were used with savagery against pickets who tried to stop the trams in the city centre. By physical means the strike was broken. [24]

Despite its defeat the strike left precisely the deep legacy of class discontent which the Unionists had feared. 100,000 people marched in the 1919 May Day demonstration in Belfast. One year later the industrial unity of 1919 spilled over into political unity. Strike leaders and other trade unionists were nominated to stand for Labour in the 1920 local elections. No less than 13 Labour candidates were elected. Significantly, in many Protestant areas, such as the Shankill Road and Sandy Road, Labour received amongst its highest percentage of the vote. Also significantly five of the thirteen newly elected Labour councillors had been members of the strike committee. Baulked on the industrial battleground, the tide of class militancy had turned to the political arena.

---

[24] *The Defence of the Realm Act (DORA) was passed in the United Kingdom on 8 August 1914, four days after the country entered the First World War, and was added to as the war progressed. It gave the government wide-ranging repressive powers and was used against the trade union and anti-war movements.*

CHAPTER EIGHT

Labour Must Wait

Not only was it in the North that the awakening of the masses had an effect in radicalising the political wing of the movement. Initially the pressure of the rank-and-file activists was placed on the leadership and the movement was driven to the left in response. It was entirely a reflection of this pressure that, in August 1918, the Irish Trade Union Congress and Labour Party, by a conference decision, changed its name to the Irish Labour Party and Trade Union Congress. The political goals of the movement were being pulled to the forefront.

This movement of the masses into action throughout Ireland had the effect of transforming the character of the national movement. The grip of Redmond was broken. His role, like that of other nationalists, in supporting the war effort, left him stranded when the tide of support for the war turned into outright opposition.

In February 1917 there came the first open sign of this transformation. A candidate from the, until then, tiny Sinn Féin organisation stood against the candidate from Redmond's party in a by–election in North Roscommon. Sinn Féin won the seat by 3,002 votes to 1,708 votes.

North Roscommon was the first clear symptom of a condition which was becoming general throughout Ireland. A general election in 1918 reduced the parliamentary party to rubble and placed radical republicans in Sinn Féin at the political head of the national struggle. Prior to 1918 the parliamentary party held 80 seats. After the election they could boast only seven, and, of these, one was in Liverpool. Sinn Féin won 73 seats, while the Unionists returned 26 of their candidates. This electoral process, reflecting the sweeping radicalisation of the country, continued throughout the immediate post-war period. By 1920, 172 councils out of 206 were under Sinn Féin control.

Redmond had fought for independence, for a separate parliament with certain powers but with recognized limitations. The switch to Sinn Féin was a switch from right-wing nationalism to petty-bourgeois radicalism and populism. No longer could limited independence be the aim. Instead the demand was for a republic. The proclamation of 1916 became enshrined as the programme of Sinn Féin.

Those elected in 1918 established their own illegal parliament in Ireland. The democratic programme of this "First Dail" was infused with populist phrases upholding in words the rights of labour. It declared that "all right to private property must be subordinate to the public right and welfare". The Irish government, it promised, would cooperate with other governments "in determining a standard of social and industrial legislation with a view to a general and lasting improvement in the conditions under which the working classes live and labour". Likewise the foremost leader of the Dail, De Valera, went out of his way to pay extensive tribute to labour and even to Connolly. Thus he could state:

"I never regarded freedom as an end in itself, but if I were asked what statement of Irish policy was most in accord with my views as to what human beings should be struggling for, I would stand side by side with James Connolly."

In words De Valera stood with Connolly at this point in time – but only to draw the support of the aroused masses. The purpose of his words was to ensure that the real ideas of Connolly were not carried into practice.

So it was with the Sinn Féin leaders as a whole. The members elected to the First Dail reflected the class content of the top of this organisation. 65 percent of its members belonged to the professional and commercial classes, mainly teachers, journalists, shopkeepers and small businessmen. It included figures such as Arthur Griffith, who had already proved himself no ally of the workers. Behind the scenes these individuals were strenuously attempting to maintain good relations with the native capitalists, with the church hierarchy and with the other "pillars" of the "Irish nation" they were in the process of creating. To use Connolly's phrase, while the old nationalist had been the "open enemies" of labour, these "radical republicans" were its "most dangerous allies".

On the one hand the radical phrases issuing from the mouths of these people reflected the leftward movement of the bottom layers of society. The ranks of Sinn Féin, and the grip it maintained, reflected the cowardly role played by the leaders of the labour movement.

While the ranks of the trade union and labour movement swung to the left and embarked on a programme of direct action, the most prominent of its leaders temporized and vacillated. Connolly was dead. Larkin was languishing in an American jail. Into the gap stepped the William O'Briens, the Thomas Johnstons and the Cathal O'Shannons. [25] With flowery speeches they echoed the sentiments of the workers. In deeds they shrank from the struggle. North and South one united class movement was developing during this period. What was required was a leadership which could tie together, in the minds of all the workers, the land and factory seizures in the South, the takeovers of towns such as Limerick, with the industrial muscle revealed by the Belfast working class in 1919. A common struggle against capitalist domination could have been begun. All the demands of the republican leadership of Sinn Féin, for a republic, for the withdrawal of the English garrison, etc., would and should have been encompassed by such a movement. But it would have gone much further. Not just for a republic, but for a workers' republic! Not just the right to have a parliament but for a revolutionary constituent assembly which could take the factories and the land out of the hands of the speculators and profiteers and place them in the hands of the working class! Not just for rule by the "Irish people" but for rule by the Irish workers, the only class capable of solving the problems of the small farmers and all the middle strata of society. Not just for independence, but for independence from British capitalism! Not just for freedom, but for freedom from exploitation! Not just against national oppression, but for socialist internationalism including the forging of the strongest possible links with the organisations of the British working class!

Such a programme, linked to decisive action on the part of the workers' organisations, could have placed labour at the head of the national struggle. By removing the fight for independence from the camp of petty-bourgeois nationalism it could have broken sectarian division and won the Protestant workers. Labour had the opportunity to intervene in this way. To do so was merely to provide the natural political extension to the industrial battles waging North and South.

At the time of the Easter rising, Sinn Féin was a tiny organisation of not more than 100 members. Within a year and a half they could boast over a quarter of a million members. Only in a revolutionary situation could such a revolutionary growth have occurred. But Sinn Féin only attracted this support because of the role of the leadership of the labour movement.

In 1916 the labour movement also was weak. However, its potential for growth was infinitely greater than that of Sinn Féin. At the bottom its ranks

---

[25.] *These were key leaders of the labour movement after the murder of James Connolly. Thomas Johnson became leader of the Irish Labour Party and an author of the programme of the first Dáil. William O'Brien emerged as leader of the ITGWU and Cathal O'Shannon was a leader of the Socialist Party of Ireland (no connection) which later split into revolutionary and reformist wings* were surging to the left, demanding action. In complete contrast the top leaders of the movement were busy only abdicating their responsibility to show a clear lead. Even those struggles which did take place did so without direction or assistance from the topmost leaders of the movement. The land seizures were carried out despite the fact that the ITGWU leaders stubbornly refused to involve their 50,000-strong agricultural labourer membership.

In political terms the labour leaders played the role of silent allies of Sinn Féin. Not only did they fail to provide a challenge to De Valera and his friends, but they gave this group every possible assistance. William O'Brien, the head of the ITGWU, actually supported and worked for the Sinn Féin candidate in one of the 1917 by-elections. Against the wishes of the rank and file of the movement, the labour leaders agreed to participate in a National Front involving the petty bourgeois nationalists. Later, Thomas Johnston, Labour Party leader, obligingly wrote a section of the programme of the First Dail for Sinn Féin. Thus he assisted in constructing the disguise by which the Sinn Féin leaders made themselves presentable to the people.

For those activists who were appalled at such decisions as the manoeuvrings of O'Brien and the other leaders, there was little opportunity to express dissent. Incredibly, despite the crescendo of class struggle, the ITGWU, the biggest union in the country, held no conference between May 1915 and August 1918. No less incredibly the executive of this union held no meeting between January 1916 and February 1918. In 1918 this policy of backsliding and outright betrayal was consummated.

In November 1918 parliament was dissolved. Labour had the opportunity to fight for the political leadership of the awakening mood of revolt. The decision of the August 1918 conference to change its name to the Labour Party and TUC showed that the ranks were squaring up for the contest. At times the workers' movement is defeated through battle. Such honourable defeats at least lay down traditions for future struggle which fresh generations will take up. But when the movement suffers defeat only because its leaders refuse to fight, all that remains is a sour taste in the mouth.

"Labour must wait." Thus De Valera instructed the Johnstons and O'Briens that they must wait their turn. "The nation" must come before any specific interest within the nation! Sinn Féin must be allowed a clear field to show the maximum unity!

At first Labour decided to fight the 1918 elections. Then they decided to accept the advice of De Valera and stand down. A special congress of the Irish Labour Party and Trade Union Congress was held and the decision not to stand was forced through against opposition from many delegates.

In a statement the leaders of the movement boasted of their generosity:

"We shall show by this action that while each of the other political parties is prepared to divide the people in their efforts to obtain power, the Irish Labour Party is the only party which is prepared to sacrifice party interests in the interests of the nation in this important crisis in the history of the nation."

For "the interests of the nation" read: the interests of the capitalists. Only they stood to benefit from Labour's gesture of "humility". The "national unity" put forward by Sinn Féin was really the unity of the Catholic toilers and small farmers marching behind the banners of the pro-capitalist parties. For this Catholic, all-class unity, Labour was asked to sacrifice the more essential unity of Catholic and Protestant workers drawing behind them the middle strata of society. It was a poor swap!

Thus it was the humble silence of Labour which allowed Sinn Féin to gain 73 of the seats in this election. Instead of a contest dominated by class interests, extending the ever-increasing industrial militancy into the political sphere, petty-bourgeois nationalism was given a free rein. As on every occasion when the national issue has been presented in any other than social terms it became a sectional and ultimately a potentially sectarian issue.

The radical nationalism of Sinn Féin could hold no attraction for the Protestant workers of the North. If rule by the De Valeras and Griffiths was the alternative to British rule and to Unionism, the traditional allegiances of the Protestants would not be broken. The task of Labour, the only body capable of drawing working-class support from the unionists, was made more difficult. As we shall see later, Carson was partially able to contain the political movement of workers within his own brand of Labour Unionism. The four genuine Labour candidates who stood in Belfast in 1918 were isolated from the labour movement throughout the country and were decisively beaten.

CHAPTER NINE

Military Repression

The post-war revolutionary upsurge affected the outlook of the British ruling class no less than it affected the labour and national movement in Ireland. During the first years of the war, with the overwhelming need to conciliate Redmond in order to draw recruits to the imperialist slaughter, Lloyd George and Asquith went to great lengths to appear to seek a solution to the problem. In addition the need to conciliate American opinion increased the government's anxiety to keep up this pretence.

After 1916 in particular, these moves represented no more than attempts to keep the Irish talking until the war ended, when the real solution would be imposed, on the tips of bayonets if necessary. Open coercion, including conscription, was not possible during the war years. Such a policy would have tied down enormous resources in Ireland, resources much needed in Europe.

Therefore Lloyd George came up with an answer – an Irish Convention in which the Irish parties and interests could meet and hammer out their own solution. Confident that no agreement could be reached between Unionists and nationalists and even among the various shades of Unionism and nationalism themselves, Lloyd George was happy to let the Convention discussions continue for as long as these parties wanted. This talking shop met on July 25, 1917 and continued to meet until April 1918. By that time the British bosses were almost in a position to let the Irish have a taste of the real solution they had in mind.

The major preoccupation of the ruling class after the war was with the threat of the socialist revolution. Should the movement on the land and in the cities, the power of the workers shown in the general strikes in the South, be harnessed with the industrial muscle shown in Belfast in 1919, and should this power in turn be linked to the might of the British workers, the capitalist system would be faced with extinction.

When the bosses looked at the republican movement they saw its radicalism, they saw the demand for a republic and nothing else, above all they saw the shadow of labour and socialism in the background.

In this climate, concessions to the Redmondites or to Sinn Féin would have been futile. One unionist explained this clearly in a letter written shortly after the 1917 North Roscommon by-election victory for Sinn Féin: "Fear was expressed that if John Redmond was put in control and had to face an election for a legislative object in that country, he would be replaced at once by Sinn Féiners, and what then? In local government elections the whole tendency is to fall to the lower stratum on each occasion." And the lowest stratum is none other than the working class. Sinn Féin might take over, and what then! These words precisely summed up the anxiety of the bosses.

A republic, to the British ruling class, was ruled out. While their prime concern was with the impetus any concession would give to the social struggle, Britain also had military strategic reasons for stamping on any other than the most limited forms of independence.

Thus when outlining terms for a settlement the British made it clear that:

"the common defence of Great Britain and Ireland in defence of their interests by land and sea shall be mutually recognized. Great Britain lives by sea-borne food, her communications depend upon the freedom of the freedom of the great sea routes."

Facilities were also required for the air force – "the Royal Air Force will need facilities for all purposes that it serves and Ireland will form an essential link in the development of air routes between the British Isles and North American continent" (*July 1921*). Particularly in relation to the strategic importance of Ireland's naval bases the war had reinforced the resolve of imperialism that there should be no concessions in this direction.

Lloyd George (*1919*) stated this conclusion in black and white terms. If in the war, he postulated,

"we had there, a land over whose harbours and inlets we had no control you might have had a situation full of peril that might well have jeopardized the life of this country. The area of submarine activity might have been extended beyond the limits of control and Britain and her allies might have been cut off from the dominions and from the USA. We cannot possibly run the risk of that, and it would be equally fatal for the interests of Ireland … I think it is right to say in the face of the demands which have been put forward from Ireland with apparent authority, that any attempt at secession will be fought with the same resolve as the Northern States of America put into the fight against the Southern States."

The demand for a republic would not be tolerated, not only because of the class danger inherent in it, but also for these military reasons. Britannia at this time might have found that she no longer "ruled the waves", if her oldest and geographically closest country were permitted to wriggle free of her clutches.

In addition British imperialism was concerned with the effect that the granting of concessions to Ireland would have on other parts of the empire. To be seen to retreat in disarray from her oldest and closest colony could have a dangerous effect on India, parts of the African continent and other already "restless" dominions.

In 1919 the first shots of the War of Independence were fired by the newly constituted Irish Republican Army (IRA). Imperialism reacted quickly by returning to their long-established method of subjugation – coercion. First with their forces already in Ireland, especially the Royal Irish Constabulary, they moved to stamp out the republican "menace". In 1919 the First Dail was suppressed. In March of that year Sir Nevil McCready was placed in command of the British forces. He had already won his spurs in the fight to uphold capitalism – in 1911, when he had let the miners at Tonypandy have a taste of his methods. [26]

A gentleman named Colonel Smith, a First World War veteran, took charge of the Royal Irish Constabulary in Munster. He revelled in his newfound opportunity to demonstrate how a people can be subdues by force. His instructions to his men were to "lie in ambush and when civilians are seen approaching shout 'hands up'. Should the order be not immediately obeyed, shoot them down." Would such a policy not result in innocent deaths? Colonel Smith had thought of this and had an answer:

"You may make mistakes occasionally and innocent people may be shot, but that cannot be helped, and you are bound to hit the right party some time. The more you shoot the better I will like you, and I assure you no policeman will get into trouble for shooting any man."

In 1920 the existing forces were supplemented by the arrival of the Black and Tans, so called because of the mixture of uniforms they wore when they arrived. The Black and Tans and the Auxiliaries have become infamous. In the true spirit of Cromwell they set about their task, and the toll of their atrocities, the sack of Cork, indiscriminate murder in Croke Park, etc., is well documented.

In 1920 a curfew was imposed in the towns. Internment was used as a

---

[26.] *Tonypandy in Wales was the scene of a bitter strike of miners in 1911, during which Churchill, as Home Secretary, ordered vicious repression* means to help break the back of the armed resistance. By 1921, 5000 republicans were interned. The generals and other army tops were consistent in their calls for a military solution. Sir Henry Wilson, chief of the general staff, perhaps summed up the attitude of these people with his call for the "shooting of Sinn Féiners by roster".

Lloyd George, among others, was a little more sensitive to the real needs of the situation. He recognized the shortcomings of a purely military solution. Such a policy might hold the situation in check. On its own it would not resolve the problem. At best it would open out a long and protracted struggle. While the IRA, with their tactics, could never inflict a military defeat on the British forces, the task of crushing them would prove both protracted and expensive. By 1920 the war in Ireland was bleeding the British Exchequer of approximately £10 million per annum.

Above all, while the war against the republicans was being waged, the class movement was developing. Clearly military coercion on its own could not prevent the movement towards land seizures, factory seizures and towards the establishment of soviets. Nor could this "contagion" of socialism, if unchecked, be prevented from infecting the population of the English cities.

A further pressure on British capital to come up with something other than mere repression came from the aroused British labour movement. Today the activities of the Provisionals, particularly the bombings of English workers in pubs, has utterly alienated the British labour movement. During the War of Independence things were very different. Then, there was real and active sympathy among British workers for the demands of the Irish.

When, in 1920, 130 Irish prisoners staged a hunger strike in Wormwood Scrubs, thousands of Irish people, together with British socialists, campaigned in support. The Liverpool dockers threatened to strike in sympathy. In 1921 a Labour Commission visited Ireland, and, upon their return, met with Lloyd George and urged that a settlement be reached. Labour meetings up and down Britain echoed the demand for a withdrawal of troops from Ireland and for an end to the use of coercive tactics against the Irish people.

This sympathy raised the fear that any advance made by the class movement in Ireland would similarly accelerate the revolutionary movement of the British workers. It was not long after the action by British workers in defence of the Wormwood Scrubs prisoners that the British working class was flexing its muscles on its own issues. 1920 saw a major strike by the miners. It saw, for example, a movement of the unemployed which brought 20,000 workers into physical battle with police in the streets of Whitehall and thereby brought the smell of revolution directly under the noses of the rulers of society.

CHAPTER TEN

Capitalism Means Division

To speed the derailment of the movement in Ireland the military coercion was spiced with the most blatant and open use of sectarianism in order to divide and weaken the workers. As in the pre-1914 crisis, and for precisely the same reasons, the antics of the Unionists were developed. Because the class threat was even more imminent, the use of sectarianism, and its encouragement by all sections of capital, was even more blatant. It was the failure of the labour movement, and the consequent dominance by petty-bourgeois nationalists in Sinn Féin, which permitted such a policy.

Partition was seized upon as an answer. Partition did not flow out of the situation within Ireland itself. As we shall see it was not imposed in order to satisfy the demands of the republican movement in the South. Rather it was forced upon the leaders of the republican movement, who were compelled by British imperialism to come to the conference table and negotiate a ceasefire on the basis of the demands of imperialism.

Nor did it develop out of the struggles of the Unionist movement within the North. It is a complete myth that the borders of the Northern Ireland state were agreed because of the determined resistance of an armed camp of Unionist reaction in the Northern counties.

Carson's armed detachments had flourished in the pre-war period. The UVF developed only on the basis of the support received from the British ruling class. Had this organisation been faced with the resistance of the tops of British society and the military machine of British imperialism, it would have disintegrated. Its aristocratic chiefs would have had no stomach for a fight against their class allies in Britain. They would have deserted at the sound of the first shot. Behind them their organisation, because of its class composition, mainly of the petty bourgeoisie and of sections of the rural population, would have disintegrated.

In a letter to Carson, written in 1915, one of the UVF leaders, Lord Dunleath, gave expression to his private forebodings at the thought of battle. To

him the fiery threats contained in the Covenant which he and his men had
signed were not to be taken too literally.

"Moreover I do not believe that our men are prepared to go into action
against any part of his Majesty's forces, and we their leaders should not
consider ourselves justified in calling upon them to do so. As I said just
now, many of us are prepared to risk a great deal for our cause, but even
our covenant does not compel us to run our heads against a wall ..."

The UVF would not have withstood any serious military resistance. But in
addition those who argue that it was the military might of Protestant reaction
which brought about partition of the country have one further "small" problem to explain. This is the fact that the UVF was virtually wiped out at the
Battle of the Somme. "Ulster" did not emerge from the armed resistance of
the Protestant population. In the post-war period, and in the years leading
up to partition, a mass army of Protestant resistance did not exist.

Certainly there were groups of armed thugs, used primarily against the
unity of the working class and the organisations of the labour movement. But
they were hardly a serious threat to the might of the British Empire!

Partition developed not out of the forces at war within Ireland. It was imposed from without by British imperialism in order to satisfy its needs at the
time. It was imposed for a clear reason, not only to draw a visible line across
the map of Ireland, but, more significantly, to draw an invisible line of bigotry
between Catholic and Protestant workers in North, between workers North
and South, and between the movement in Ireland and that in Britain.

During the pre-war crisis when the idea of partition had been raised the
Unionists had been no more in favour of it than had their nationalist oppo-
nents. At that time partition, when posed, was merely used as a ruse to defeat
Home Rule as a whole.

Carson and his Tory bands followed a similar strategy when they concentrated their efforts on the north east of the country. There and there alone it
was possible for their ideas to gain a base beyond the layers of privilege at
the top of society. Thus, in 1913, Carson was prepared to threaten to establish
a provisional government in Ulster if Home Rule became a reality. Behind
such fiery declarations, behind the saber-rattling of military-style parades and
behind the frantic efforts to gather signatures for the Covenant lay the belief
that Ulster was the rock on which this and every Home Rule attempt would
founder.

Time after time Carson made his position clear: "if Ulster succeeds

Home Rule is dead. Home Rule is impossible without Belfast and the surrounding parts as a portion of the scheme." Or the following statement contained in a letter he wrote to the Irish Times in October 1912:

"not even Mr. Redmond could undertake the government of Ireland without being able to draw upon the resources of Ulster and the prosperity won by the energy and capacity of Ulstermen."

Not until 1916, and then only after extreme pressure from Lloyd George, did Carson reluctantly accept the concept of partition. Even then, his acceptance resulted in further dissension and division among his supporters.

The "tactic" of leaning on the support of Ulster employed by Carsonites prior to 1914 was handed back by the British government as a "policy" in the post-war period. The Government of Ireland Act of 1920 proposed two separate parliaments, one for the North and one for the South. It was accompanied with the threat that, if it would not work, the alternative was colonial government for Ireland.

The real purpose of this policy of division was soon clear. Partition was to be accompanied with a major campaign aimed at re-injecting the poison of sectarian division into the minds of the workers. As in 1906, when one reactionary had been able to comment that Unionism was dead among the masses, so after 1918 the ideas of socialism were developing apace among Protestant and Catholic workers. Sectarianism was used to reverse this process.

Once again the utterances of the Unionists give the clearest indication of the extent to which class ideas were destroying their grip on the situation. Dawson Bates, in 1919, in a letter to Captain C.C. Craig, Unionist MP for South Armagh, gave a glimpse of the desperation of the Unionists at the rise of labour. In different words but in the same dire tone, he repeated the message of Crawford of thirteen years earlier: that Unionism is dead among the masses. "There is a general desire to kick against all authority and all discipline all over the three kingdoms." Bates was astute enough to realize the electoral consequences of this general revolt: "the Labour question is becoming acute in Belfast and the North of Ireland and egged on by nationalists, many of the electors are finding fault with their respective associations in the various districts."

If the labour leaders in Ireland were not aware of their own strength, the Unionists were not so blind. They recognized the power of the class movement to dissolve their working-class base of support. To counteract this danger the Ulster Unionists Labour Association was formed in June 1918. President of this supposed working-class association was the champion of the workers' cause – Carson himself!

In December 1918 the general election was fought. Carson, it is said, went to the lengths of refusing to cooperate with his colleagues unless three of the nine Unionist candidates in Belfast were trade unionists.

Why? Because Carson was anxious to ensure representation for the workers? On the contrary! Carson sought to present an impression of all-class representation in order to disguise the reality of the vicious anti-working-class nature of unionism.

Three token trade-unionists were chosen, principally to halt the drift to real workers' representation. Significantly these three "workers" who were offered the "privilege" of standing with their aristocratic rulers and "betters" were all skilled workers, probably filled with craft prejudices. One was a shipwright, one a tenter and one a lithographic printer. When elected, these three, even though drawn from the labour aristocracy, mixing with the lords and ladies of the British establishment at Westminster, became among the most degenerate of all the Unionist representatives, mere tokens, cardboard replicas of workers, toadies pulled forward and told to speak and behave like workers in order to please their masters.

The elevating of such stooges could not stop the irresistible drive of the working class towards independent action. Only weeks after the election of these people and of the better-heeled versions of Unionism, Belfast was virtually under the control of the working class. And the Unionists found themselves powerless to intervene. The conclusion, again clearly expressed by Dawson Bates, was that the influence of the Ulster Unionist Labour Association would have to be extended. Writing to Carson in June 1919 he complained that the:

"all class organisations, the parliamentary associations and the Orange Institutions do not find time to discuss matters which might better attract working people. The absence of such discussions frequently leads to the younger members of the working classes joining socialist and extreme organisations run by the Independent Labour Party where they were educated in views very different to those held by our body. The defect has to a very large extent been made good by the Ulster Unionist Labour Association, but at the same time it is felt that having ordinary meetings, such as they have about once a month, is not sufficient. In other words, the Association will have to extend its sphere of operations".

Smother the workers with sectarianism! Cultivate a labour identity in order to drag the workers away from those socialist organisations which were fighting to remedy such conditions! This was the role of the Unionists, particularly through the Ulster Unionist Labour Association. Bates is quite explicit about this.

"it is felt that it is desirable that this Association should extend its operations so as to afford a greater opportunity to the working classes to belong to it and so prevent them from joining political Labour organisations whose primary object may be the advancement of Home Rule."

Thus is unequivocally stated the real basis and use of sectarianism – to prevent the development of the socialist movement.

Yet despite all these efforts the labour movement continued to develop. The January 1920 corporation elections resulted in the return of 13 Labour candidates from the Labour Party and the Independent Labour Party. Labour Unionists also stood in an attempt to maintain the bridle of sectarianism on the workers. Only six Labour Unionists were returned. No less than ten trade-union officials were elected.

Nor was this a movement exclusive to the north east of Ireland at this time. Despite the fact that Labour had not intervened in the previous election in 1918, and despite the fact that the leaders of the labour movement had failed to place themselves at the head of the revolt developing within Ireland, the elections held in 1920 throughout the country revealed the basis of potential support which existed for Labour. In total in Ireland in these elections, of the 1806 seats, 550 Sinn Féin councillors were elected. 355 Unionists were returned. 238 nationalists, 108 ratepayers' candidates and 161 independents were also elected. Labour despite the failings of its leaders, managed to win 394 seats. In this result is clearly seen the potential of Labour to develop as the major political force within society.

Clearly more desperate measures from the bigots would be required if the menace of "workers' unity" was to be put to an end. The "extension of the operations" of groups like the UULA and the Unionist leaders was soon apparent. Every conceivable method was used to infect the shop floor with sectarianism. Inflammatory speeches encouraging pogroms were made. The employers showed their hand. An extreme sectarian group, the Belfast Protestant Association, was given permission by many employers to hold meetings in the workplaces. In July 1920 this incitement came to a head with the outbreak of bitter violence against Catholics and socialists mainly in Belfast.

By the third week of July serious rioting had broken out and it didn't take long before it spread into the shipyards. There, Catholic workers were driven into the Lagan and pounded with steel rivets (Belfast confetti!). These attacks on the shipyard workforce were launched from the outside. Gangs of Protestant thugs, many from the rural and semi-rural areas outside Belfast, attacked the gates of the yards.

Protestant Unionists soon intervened to fan these flames of sectarianism. One called for a show of revolvers in the shipyard. James Craig, soon to become the foremost figure of Ulster Unionism, in a comment directed at the shipyard men declared "if you ask me my opinion of your action I say well done." Likewise Carson, a few days after the riots, considered the time was ripe to announce that he was "prouder of my friends in the shipyard than of any other friends I have in the world".

The pogroms spread to other factories and beyond into working-class estates. Outside Belfast, in Lisburn and Banbridge, riots resulted in the expulsion of almost all of the Catholic families living there. Significantly not only Catholics but also socialists and active trade-unionists were driven from their jobs and homes.

At the end of this upheaval there was not one Catholic working in the shipyard. This is common knowledge. Not so well known is the fact that an estimated 25 percent of those expelled were Protestants, in other words at least a quarter of the victims of their pogrom suffered as socialists and trade union activists.

Such atrocities were given the backing not only of the political heads of Unionism but of the representatives of capital. No protection was given to the Catholic workers by state forces. In fact it was at this time that the British government came up with its proposal that a special constabulary should be established – in other words that Protestant gangs should be given the stamp of official approval and should receive uniforms and arms.

The capitalist state is not the protector of the interests of the working class. This was again shown in these activities. The workers have only themselves and their organisations to fall back upon. In this period there were many honourable incidents where Protestant socialists and trade unionists attempted to intervene to halt the pogroms. The advanced layers of the workers were repulsed and made an open stand in defence of the expelled workers.

The National Union of Railwaymen in a resolution at a conference in Belfast stated:

"without complete unity amongst the working classes, (we should not allow either religious or political differences to prevent their emancipation) which can be achieved through a great international brotherhood the world over, no satisfactory progress could be made."

A delegation from the Amalgamated Society of Carpenters and Joiners spoke to the shipyard workers, attempting to defuse the situation. They went so far as to produce a blacklist of firms from which expulsions had taken place. This included the Workman and Clarke shipyard, the Sirrocco plant and union executive, while a further 2,000, by staying at work, were expelled from the union.

It was the lack of an overall lead from the trade unions and from the labour movement generally throughout Britain and Ireland which determined that such courageous but isolated calls could not be successful. Without the support and active backing of workers' organisations throughout the British Isles such calls were in fact foolhardy. At that time there were approximately 100,000 people in the area that was to become Northern Ireland who had no jobs. The labour organisations were not conducting a decisive struggle in Ireland around socialist policies and for jobs. It was therefore not surprising that 2000 members of the Amalgamates Society should have been reluctant to risk their livelihood and support their union.

The role of the republican movement was no help to the attempt of the labour organisations to call a halt to the bloodshed. The pogroms in the North were answered by the IRA with the boycott of Ulster goods. Later this boycott was ratified by the Dail.

Opposition from the labour movement was one thing. If strong enough it could have isolated the bigots. Opposition from the petty-bourgeois nationalists was something totally different. The stronger it was, the more it reinforced the influence of bigots over the minds of Protestant workers.

Until July 1920 the labour movement in the North had been going forward. Industrially and then politically it was moving from strength to strength. The 19 July pogroms and the passing of the Government of Ireland Act threw this process into reverse gear. The potential which had existed, for the movement to develop as never before, was temporarily lost.

In the period before 1914 the labour movement North and South had recognized the dangers inherent in partition. Leaders like Connolly concluded that only action by the workers' organisations could avert disaster. At that time the weakness of the movement lay in its youth, in the fact that it had engaged in a series of exhausting industrial battles. Connolly and other leaders strove to overcome these objective handicaps. Under the then existing conditions he and the other leaders of the movement faced an uphill battle.

From the war the movement emerged fresh, the scars of battle healed, and on the crest of a revolutionary wave. Its body was invigorated. But its brain was sadly weakened. Had Labour intervened in the 1918 election the forces of the working class would have been drawn together North and South. Workers would have lined up against sectarianism and against reaction in all its forms. Had the leaders of the movement launched a campaign for socialism from that time, taking it to every workshop, to every estate, they would have won the leadership of the national struggle. In the years after 1918 they failed to face up to this task. Had they done so the radicalisation of the country would not have mustered around the banner of mere nationalism. It would have been a struggle for socialism North, South and in Britain also.

From the criminal decision not to participate in 1918, and the subsequent lack of a campaign around any independent class programme, stemmed the defeats suffered North and South in the early 1920s. That decision, that inaction, left the advanced workers in the North isolated in 1920 when the bigots drew their swords. Had the movement not sat back and allowed petty-bourgeois nationalists to tap the revolutionary energy of the masses, partition itself could have been averted.

The Government of Ireland Act was foisted on Ireland by British imperialism primarily in order to divide and disorientate the workers' movement in Ireland and in Britain. It gave legitimacy to the activities of the Carsonite thugs in the North. It assisted the attempts of such reactionaries to break up the solidarity shown in 1919. And with the temporary paralysis of the workers' organisations in the North, the ruling class were more able to concentrate their efforts on the southern parts of the country. Coercion was intensified and, at all times, the pressure maintained on the leadership of the republican movement to force them to come to terms.

It was the petty-bourgeois nature of this leadership which opened a way to a settlement – on the terms of imperialism, of course. The British government through Lloyd George pressed for negotiations to take place. On July 11, 1921 a truce was called. De Valera led a delegation to London to discuss terms. What they were offered amounted to a mere sham of token independence, approximately the proposals contained in previous Home Rule Bills, though spiced with a few additional concessions. Air and naval facilities were to be granted to Britain, and recruiting would still take place in Ireland for the British army. There was to be a limitation on the size of the Irish army. And on top of this the recognition of the Northern Ireland parliament, and with it the division of the country, was demanded.

De Valera rejected these proposals. However, in his correspondence it was made quite clear that some form of compromise might yet be reached. The struggle of the Irish masses was to be reduced to a game of swapping concessions with the representatives of British capital.

In October a fresh delegation, this time led by Arthur Griffith and excluding De Valera, went to negotiate with Lloyd George. The central objections to the British proposals raised by this delegation were the question of Ulster, and also the issue of the wording of an oath of allegiance to the British monarch. The military conditions were fairly readily accepted.

During the negotiations it became clear that the latter-day Daniel O'Connell, Arthur Griffith, was the most susceptible to the persuasive methods of Lloyd George. When the proposal to establish a Boundary Commission to determine where exactly the border would run was made, and when a modified version of the oath of allegiance was produced, it was apparent that Griffith was prepared to capitulate.

Lloyd George seized upon the cracks appearing among the Irish delegation and bluntly informed them that if they did not sign the treaty the British would embark on a course of all-out war "within three days". Griffith had already given a personal assurance that he would sign no matter what his colleagues would do. But they were not long in following suit.

There is no doubt that Lloyd George's threat of all-out war was no bluff. Had the treaty not been accepted, a savage offensive against the republican forces would have been begun. This was being seriously considered by the capitalists as the first part of a direct offensive against the working class. The leaders of the British military machine had been demanding an extension of their powers and of their operations in Ireland. For example, the commander of the forces, Sir Henry Wilson, had demanded powers "to intern anyone without charge or trial for an indefinite period, and the power to try any prisoner by court-martial and without legal advice, except in cases requiring the death penalty." Had the republican leaders not been prepared to accept the terms being offered at this stage, imperialism would have no choice but to continue to escalate the military efforts in order to enforce these leaders to the conference table and to compromise at some future stage.

For their part the republican leaders agreed to the British terms firstly because ingrained within them and their class outlook was the spirit of compromise, but secondly, and more importantly, because they could see no prospect of victory. Of all the republican leaders few were more closely in touch with the actual military situation as was Michael Collins. Collins himself, in 1921, estimated that the IRA had only 2000-3000 men whom they could rely upon at any one time. In addition, their operations were being handicapped by a severe shortage of ammunition.

Only one force could have led a successful struggle against imperialism – the working class. The De Valeras, Griffiths etc., had no perspective for the mobilisation of the workers. Their prominence was one of the factors repelling the Protestant workers in the North. History books tell us that the treaty arose from "the betrayal" of a few individuals. On the contrary! The need to come to terms arose from the methods that had been adopted by the leaders of the struggle in Ireland. Above all, it arose from the backsliding of the labour leadership in 1918 and soon afterwards.

The republican struggle was divorced from the social agitations welling up at the time. "Labour must wait" meant that the demands of the working class were dismissed. By pressing their interests the workers were said to be "endangering" the unity of the republican forces! On the land also, the tenants were seizing the estates only to find themselves remonstrated by Sinn Féin and the IRA, who even went to the lengths of carrying out evictions in order to break the back of the land-seizure movement.

Pushing the social struggle to the background, Sinn Féin inevitably leaned towards the capitalists and away from the working class. In so doing it drained the struggle of the resources and reserves required to ensure success.

In addition, the methods of struggle which were adopted, those of a campaign of individual terror as conducted by the forces of the IRA, were incapable of defeating imperialism. History, drawn from the international experience of the working class, teaches that it is only mass action by the organisations of the working class which can change society. The truth of this was shown in Ireland during these years. Had a treaty not been negotiated in 1921, the IRA campaign could have been continued, but it would not have achieved the military and economic expulsion of imperialism. On the basis of the methods which had been adopted up to 1921, of guerrilla activity, there could have been only one result of such a campaign – ultimate defeat and a settlement of some sort chiefly on the bosses' terms.

It was the objective factors bearing down upon the republican movement, stemming from their false strategy, from their false policies, and also from the failures of the labour movement, which forced the compromise terms of the treaty to be accepted. The subjective factors, the willingness to compromise and betray inherent in the psychology and cringing class outlook of these petty-bourgeois leaders, merely accelerated this process.

The treaty was not a sudden and unexpected "betrayal" of a few individuals. It was the only possible consequence of the methods of struggle adopted and the social composition of the forces involved. No matter what individuals were conducted, nothing could get away from the fact that the cause itself was being squeezed by events towards shabby compromise.

Labour and working-class unity were the real victims of partition. Labour alone could have averted this menace. The all-Irish unity of the working class continues to be a victim of the political division of the country. But just as only labour could have averted partition in 1920 – so only united class action struggling for socialism can end partition today.

Appendix:

The Real Ideas of James Connolly
By Peter Hadden, in 2006, on the 90th
anniversary of Connolly's execution

I t is necessary because, with this year's anniversary celebrations of the
1916 Easter Rising, we are likely to witness the nauseating spectacle of
Irish government representatives, leaders of the establishment parties
in the south along with the main nationalist parties in the north, trying to
commemorate and venerate Connolly as though, somehow, they follow in
his tradition.

Connolly, were he alive today, would be fighting as relentlessly against
these people and the system they represent as he fought against their equiv-
alents in Ireland and internationally in his own time. But he would not be
surprised that people who are the enemies of all that he stood for would try
to claim his political heritage. After all, in the centenary year of the 1798
Rebellion, Connolly noted the way the establishment of the time did much
the same to the memory of United Irish leader, Wolfe Tone. "Apostles of
freedom", he wrote in the first edition of his newspaper, Workers Republic,
"are ever idolised when dead, but crucified when living".

Connolly was born in the Cowgate district of Edinburgh in 1868, the
youngest of three sons. His father was a carter and the family lived in extreme poverty. James had to work from the age of ten or eleven. He worked
in a printers, a bakery and a mosaic tiling factory. His education was rudi-
mentary and his formidable skills in writing – not just his political and historical journalism but also his attempts to get a message across through
poetry and drama – were largely self taught. Desmond Greaves, in his bi-
ography of Connolly, surmises that the young James had to read by the light
of embers, "whose charred sticks served him as pencils". Hence his slight
squint. Connolly was also slightly bow legged as a result of rickets, a common by-product of poverty and malnourishment.

He was only 14 when poverty forced him to adopt a pseudonym and enlist with the King's Liverpool Regiment of the British Army. His service took him to Ireland and lasted almost seven years before he deserted and returned to Scotland at the end of 1888 or early in 1889. It was then that, scraping by through casual work in Edinburgh, Connolly began his lifelong involvement in socialist politics. He joined the Socialist League, a split from the Social Democratic Federation (SDF), one of the earliest socialist groups in Britain. Members of the Socialist League included Eleanor Marx, daughter of Karl Marx, and one of its main influences was Frederick Engels.

All the groups that existed at the time were very loose and federal in structure and there was a constant overlap in membership. By the time he left Scotland in 1896 to take up an invitation to become the secretary of the Dublin Socialist Club, Connolly, although in financial destitution, was the secretary of the Scottish Socialist Federation and of the Scottish Labour Party, the local name for Kier Hardie's Independent Labour Party (ILP).

Within months of his arrival in Dublin he converted the Dublin Socialist Club into the much more organised Irish Socialist Republican Party (ISRP), formed at a meeting of eight people in a bar in Dublin's Thomas Street in May 1896. He became its paid organiser at a salary of £1 a week. From that time until his execution twenty years later, Connolly was a full-time revolutionary, working, when the money was there, for small socialist groups like the ISRP or later the Socialist Party of Ireland, or else as an outstanding trade union organiser. For much of this time Connolly and his family continued to live in poverty. Much of the time he was forced to go on prolonged speaking tours to raise funds, to Scotland, England and the USA.

Connolly understood the need for publications to get his ideas across. He produced a number of important pamphlets and published a number of newspapers, notably Workers Republic, first launched as an ISRP publication, and The Harp, a newspaper he first issued in the US, where he lived from 1903-1910.

Maintaining these papers on a shoe string and with a limited circulation would not have been possible but for the gargantuan energies Connolly poured into the task. He was the main contributor, the person who ensured that publication dates were met, printers' bills paid, and was most often the driving force on sales. Bearing out that the job of revolutionaries is to do what needs to be done, no matter how mundane the task, Connolly took it on himself to see that his papers reached the widest working-class audience. In the US he stood at street corners and outside meetings selling The Harp. One of the early pioneers of the US labour movement, Elizabeth Gurley

Flynn, in her autobiography, remembers Connolly pushing the sales of this journal: "It was a pathetic sight to see him standing, poorly clad, at the door of Cooper Union or some other East Side Hall, selling his little paper". It was through his articles in these journals and in the papers of other organisations that Connolly developed the ideas that he held most consistently through his life. He took the ideas of Marx and Engels, especially their view that the motor force of history is the struggle between contending classes, and applied them to Ireland.

His earliest pamphlet, a series of essays published in 1897 under the title, Erin's Hope, drew the conclusion that Connolly defended and expanded upon throughout his life, that the Irish working class was "the only secure foundation on which a free nation can be built". This conclusion was amplified and presented in a more rounded form in his major work, the 1910 pamphlet Labour in Irish History. This booklet remains Connolly's most important contribution in the realm of ideas.

The main conclusion of Labour in Irish History is that the Irish middle and propertied class "have a thousand economic strings in the shape of investments binding them to English capitalism". It follows that "only the Irish working class remain as the incorruptible inheritors of the fight for freedom in Ireland". These conclusions parallel the ideas being developed by Leon Trotsky at the time, now known as the theory of the permanent revolution.

Trotsky explained that the native bourgeois (capitalist class) in the less developed countries and in the colonial world had emerged late onto the scene of history. They were too enfeebled as a class to dare to put themselves at the head of movements to remove the last vestiges of feudalism or establish independent nation states as the bourgeois in the established capitalist powers had, nervously and often incompletely, managed to do. These tasks fell then to the working class who, in taking power, would carry through the unfinished tasks that in a previous historical period had fallen to the rising capitalist class. But at same time the working class would proceed, uninterrupted, to carry through the tasks of the socialist revolution.

Connolly never drew these conclusions with the precision of Trotsky. Nor had he the opportunity to read Trotsky's material. As with many of his other writings, there is occasional ambiguity in his writings on the national question, an ambiguity that was amplified by his actions at the end of his life. He did make statements, especially at that time, which could be read as supporting the idea that independence would give a boost to the struggle for socialism. For example, in 1916 he commented that independence is "the first requisite for the free development of the national powers needed for our class". Loose formulations like this have been used by some on the left to back the mistaken notion that national independence is somehow a necessary first 'stage' on the road to socialism and to justify alliances with nationalists to achieve this.

This was never really Connolly's view. His most consistent material states the opposite. In Labour in Irish History and in his other main writings on the national question, he is more or less at one with Trotsky; that it is the working class who must achieve independence and, in so doing, will also establish socialism. This made him a giant of his time.

In many other respects Connolly stood politically head and shoulders above those around him in the British and Irish labour movement. He recognised that "every political party is the party of a class" which it uses "to create and maintain the conditions most favourable to its own class rule". The working class needed its own political instrument and this instrument should stand independent of other parties.

It goes without saying what his position would have been on the present day calls of trade union leaders for 'social partnership'; on those like the Irish Labour Party and Sinn Féin who spend their time knocking on the doors of the right-wing establishment parties seeking coalition government; or indeed on those on the left who quietly drop their socialist ideas so they can participate in broad 'fronts' with individuals and groups that are fervently hostile to socialism.

The socialist organisations of Connolly's time were still mainly propaganda organisations without a mass political base or influence. To Connolly this was something to be changed and the question of the hour was how to build them into mass organisations without diluting their socialist content. Intense debates on questions like this raged within all the socialist groupings that Connolly was involved with. There were often very bitter exchanges that reflected different political trends that were emerging. One of his political experiences was with the Scottish wing of the SDF, ultimately a propagandist sect, led by Henry Hyndman, a man whose role, as Connolly saw it, was "to preach revolution and practice compromise and to do neither thoroughly".

When he left Ireland for the US in 1903, Connolly joined the Socialist Labour Party (SLP) which was led by Daniel De Leon. Connolly soon clashed with De Leon over a number of theoretical questions and more particularly over the dictatorial way in which he ran the SLP. De Leon's response was not always political – among other things he accused Connolly of being a

"Jesuit agent" and a "police spy". All in all it was a bitter experience and Connolly would have agreed with Engels who, early in the 1890s, wrote that the SDF and SLP treated Marxism in a "doctrinaire and dogmatic way as something to be learnt off by heart... To them it is a credo and not a guide to action".

Connolly left the SLP in 1908 declaring it had no future in De Leon's hands, except as a "church". He joined the Socialist Party, a larger organisation but with a more compromising/reformist outlook, in order to "be one of the revolutionary minority within it". This demonstrates his total absence of political sectarianism. He knew the importance of clear ideas but he also understood that it was necessary to take those ideas into the living movement of the working class, not refrigerate them in a pure political sect.

At the 1912 Irish Trades Union Congress, held in Clonmel, it was Connolly who successfully moved the motion for independent labour represen tation that marked the birth of the Irish Labour Party. He saw no contradiction between this and his work to build his own Socialist Party of Ireland. Connolly, in other words, instinctively understood the dual task of socialists to encourage, assist and participate in every development that draws the broad mass of workers into political activity, while at the same time building a more conscious socialist organisation.

This does not mean that he had a clear conception of the need for a revolutionary party that could act as the instrument of the working class in carrying through the socialist revolution. At the time, only Lenin in Russia understood that a successful revolution would require a conscious leadership organised in such a way that it would not bend politically under the pressures of events.

Trade union struggles

Connolly, like most of the Marxists of his day, was not fully clear what instrument the working class would use to overthrow capitalism or how. For a time, he put forward the syndicalist view that the main role would be played by industrial unions. His flirtation with syndicalism does not mean that he saw no role for politics or parties. Throughout his life he was consistent on the need for the working class to organise itself politically as well as industrially.

Connolly understood the critical importance of ideas. But he would never have been content to play the role of a dusty, De Leon style, professor. He understood that theory is only a preparation for action and that the only real testing ground for ideas is in the living movement. During the last decade of his life in particular, most of which he spent working as a revolutionary trade union organiser, his ideas and his methods were put into practice in a series of momentous struggles and upheavals.

His ability as a mass workers' leader was put to the test in Ireland in 1911 when he became the Belfast organiser of James Larkin's Irish Transport and General Workers Union (ITGWU). He had returned from the US with several years' experience working as an organiser for the Industrial Workers of the World. During this time, he had participated in some of the bloody battles that were being fought by US workers against vicious bosses backed by armed police and scabs.

Connolly took up his position in the ITGWU just as an explosive wave of strikes was taking place in Britain and Ireland. Three million strike days were lost in 1909. Three years later the figure was 41 million. Ireland saw the most bitter battles as employers tried to forcibly resist the militant growth of New Unionism, the organisation of the semi-skilled and unskilled, in the form of the ITGWU. In 1911 Connolly led a struggle of the Belfast dockers. That was quickly followed by an approach from female mill workers, the "linen slaves of Belfast", and an inspiring strike by more than 1,000 of these workers against the grim conditions and tyrannical managerial regime they suffered in the mills.

At the end of 1911 Connolly had to go to Wexford where ITGWU members had been locked out since August in an attempt by employers to break the union. During this dispute, the workers formed a defence organisation, a 'Workers Police', to protect themselves from the police. This was a forerunner of the Irish Citizens' Army which was formed for the same reason during the 1913 Dublin lock out.

Dublin 1913 was the culmination of this period in which the forces of labour and capital went head to head in Ireland. In August 1913, the Dublin Employers' Association, led by William Martin Murphy, locked out ITGWU members, demanding they leave the union. This was a bid to finally break the back of the Irish labour movement before a Home Rule parliament was established.

The struggle dragged on until the end of January 1914 when the workers were finally starved back to work. At its highpoint, it involved virtually the whole of the Dublin working class. The undisputed leaders of the workers were Larkin and Connolly. Arraigned against them were not just the employers and the forces of the capitalist state, but the churches and the forces of right-wing nationalism. Lenten pastorals from the pulpits denounced socialism and trade unionism. The Ancient Order of Hibernians

– Ancient Order of Hooligans to Connolly – who from the early days of the ISRP had been involved in repeated attempts to physically break up Connolly's meetings and rallies, broke into the Irish Worker printing office and smashed the type.

In the end it was the false friends rather than the open enemies of the ITGWU who left the workers of Dublin isolated and with little choice but to return to work. Connolly and Larkin had called for a solidarity general strike in Britain and for the blacking of the scab boats that were delivering goods in and out of the port of Dublin. The issue of blacking was debated at a special meeting of the British TUC in December but, with the leaders of the main unions opposed to solidarity action, the motion was decisively defeated by 2,280,000 votes to 203,000.

The eventual return-to-work was on the employers' terms but the immediate victory they had won was at the cost of laying down a tradition of militancy and solidarity which meant that the union had been badly wounded but not broken.

The national question

This was one of three defeats suffered by the working-class movement in the space of a few short years, which without a doubt left Connolly somewhat disorientated and shaped the direction he took in the last three years of his life.

Connolly's return to Belfast after the strike was against the backcloth of the Home Rule crisis of 1912-14. The proposal by Westminster to grant limited Home Rule to Ireland had invoked a furious opposition among Unionists and from a significant section of the British ruling class. The Ulster Volunteer Force was formed in 1913 and the Unionist hierarchy voted to establish a provisional government in Ulster in the event of the Home Rule Bill becoming law. With the drums of civil war beating loudly a compromise was arrived at that allowed for the 'temporary' exclusion of any of the Ulster counties that chose to stay out of the arrangement. Nationalist leader, John Redmond, accepted this deal.

Connolly dismissed the idea that this exclusion would be temporary and correctly viewed these events as a defeat for the working class. He predicted that partition would "mean a carnival of reaction both North and South, would set back the Irish labour movement, and paralyse all advanced movements while it endured".

During his time in Belfast, Connolly had attempted to unite workers both industrially and politically. But he did not manage to give the unity achieved in strikes and other struggles a lasting organisational form. The ITGWU organised Catholic workers in the main, as did the socialist political groups with which he was involved.

Connolly stood for class unity and fought to achieve it, but this fine ambition in itself was not enough to break the sectarian mould. He never properly examined the reasons why big sections of the Protestant working class were prepared to fall in behind the Lords and Ladies of Unionism. If he had looked more closely he would have seen that Protestant workers had real fears about what might happen under a Home Rule parliament and would have understood that it was necessary for socialists to put forward ideas to counter those fears.

The greater Belfast area was the industrial hub of Ireland at the time. The heavy industries that had developed were part of an industrial triangle whose other two points were Liverpool and Glasgow. Protestant workers had developed strong ties of struggle with workers in these cities especially. Their fear was that in a Home Rule parliament, run in the interests of the smaller businesses in the south who favoured protectionist measures, their ties with the labour movement in Britain would be broken and their jobs would be threatened as their industries were cut off from their export markets.

Connolly's analysis of the national question as it had evolved in Ireland was fundamentally correct, but his application of that analysis in the form of a programme was somewhat one-sided and, as such, would not re-assure the mass of Protestants. Along with Larkin, he stood for separate Irish trade unions as well as separate political organisations. This was necessary in order to draw Catholic workers away from the Nationalists. But in the north it created the danger, as actually happened, that Protestants would, by and large, stay with the British organisations and workers would be divided along religious lines. At the very least, it would have been necessary to advocate that special formal links be maintained between the working class organisations in Ireland and in Britain, and especially to defend and maintain the ties that had been built up between shop stewards' organisations.

Likewise on the question of independence. Connolly was correct in advocating an Irish Socialist Republic, but this too was posed in a one-sided manner. When Marx spoke about the struggle for Irish independence, meaning independence on a capitalist basis, he added the rider that after independence "may come federation". Connolly's material leaves this idea to the side.

While fighting to place the labour movement, with its goal of a socialist republic, at the head of the struggle for independence, it would have been better if Connolly had also argued to maintain the links with the British working class and had put forward as the ultimate objective the idea of a voluntary socialist federation of Ireland and Britain.

World war & the Easter rising

The third defeat suffered by the working class came in the form of the outbreak of war in August 1914. Before the war, the mighty parties of the Second International, particularly the Social Democratic Party of Germany, had issued belligerent anti-war statements and had promised a general strike to paralyse the war effort should hostilities be announced.

When the fighting started, all this resistance, with the exception of some courageous individual leaders and of a few parties like the Russian Bolsheviks, crumbled away to nothing. To Connolly this was another blow and he responded in his typical vituperative style: "What then becomes of all our resolutions, all our protests of fraternisation, all our threats of general strikes, all our carefully built machinery of internationalism, all our hopes for the future? Were they all as sound and fury, signifying nothing?"

The outbreak of war was accompanied by a wave of jingoism. Class ideas along with strikes and other expressions of class struggle were, for the moment, pushed to the background. In Ireland, Nationalist leader John Redmond, became a voluntary recruiting sergeant for the British army and tens of thousands who had previously drilled in the uniforms of the Irish volunteers joined up.

It is clear from Connolly's writings after 1914 that all these disappointments and betrayals affected him deeply. His writings on the war, as a whole, were not so clear and precise as earlier works. At bottom he maintained his socialist and internationalist outlook but, increasingly, his ideas became tempered by his frustration at the passivity of the working class in face of the slaughter in Europe: "Even an unsuccessful attempt at social revolution by force of arms, following the paralysis of the economic life of militarism, would be less disastrous to the Socialist cause than the act of Socialists allowing themselves to be used in the slaughter of their brothers in the cause. A great continental uprising of the working class would stop the war".

With England so heavily preoccupied, he began to consider that the first blow could be struck in Ireland. As the war bogged down to the seemingly interminable horror of the trenches, the need to act quickly to ensure that this blow was struck became his overriding concern.

In his impatience he was prepared to set some of the ideas and methods he had so carefully developed during a lifetime of revolutionary struggle temporarily to the side. In Labour and Irish History he points out correctly that "revolutions are not the product of our brains, but of ripe material conditions". In an earlier Shan Van Vocht article he criticised the Young Irelanders and Fenians for taking to the field when the conditions for revolution had not matured: "The Young Irelanders made no reasonable effort to prepare the popular mind for revolution so failure was inevitable". Now he stressed the opposite argument, criticising those in the Young Ireland movement who talked about revolution but when the time came "began to make excuses, to murmur about the danger of premature insurrection".

With the working class largely quiescent, Connolly looked to the radical nationalist forces then organised in the Irish Republican Brotherhood (IRB) and the 13,000 Irish Volunteers who had broken from Redmond over his support for the war. He hoped that an uprising in Ireland, even if it was organised for nationalist rather than socialist objectives would, as he put it, "set the torch to a European conflagration that will not burn out until the last throne and the last capitalist bond and debenture will be shrivelled on the funeral pyre of the last war lord".

In order to pressurise the IRB, and through them the Volunteers, into action, Connolly was prepared to make political concessions he would not have made at any other time in his life. He was fully correct to work alongside the nationalists in opposition to the war as he did in the Irish Neutrality League. But in joining hands on specific issues it was also necessary, as Connolly had done throughout his life, to maintain an organisational and political independence. Connolly never abandoned his socialist ideas but there were times when, by not putting them forward, he allowed his views to be blurred with those of the nationalists. It was the green flag of independence, not the red flag of socialism, not even his own Starry Plough, that he flew over Liberty Hall, the ITGWU headquarters.

The conditions for a successful rising did not exist in 1916. From this point of view the rising was premature and doomed to failure from the start. Connolly was aware of this. When, on the morning of the rising his long-term colleague William O'Brien passed him on the stairs of Liberty Hall and asked if there was any chance of success, Connolly's reply was "none whatsoever".

For Connolly its purpose was as an act of military defiance whose repercussions would hopefully reverberate around the other European nations and encourage the working class of other countries to rise. His lack of any real attempt to use his position at the head of the ITGWU to prepare the working class to back the rising shows that he was only too well aware that there was no broad mood of support for what he was about to do. He made no call for a general strike to paralyse the movement of troops and munitions. During the rising itself he made no attempt to appeal to the British troops on a class basis not to fight.

Leaving aside the issue of whether it was correct to go ahead at this time, the manner in which Connolly participated was also wrong. In his desperation to make sure that the rising went ahead he agreed to participate largely on the political terms of the Volunteers, rather than his own.

He put his name to the Proclamation of the Irish Republic which was read by Pádraic Pearse from the steps of the GPO. The proclamation is a straightforward statement of nationalist, not socialist ideas. It is true that there are phrases in it that were most probably insisted on by Connolly, such as the declaration of "the right of the people of Ireland to the ownership of Ireland". Connolly had previously always sternly opposed the idea of an appeal to the "whole people", which includes the "rack renting landlords" and the "profit-grinding capitalists" and based himself on the interests of the working class.

In the run up to and during the rising he issued no separate platform setting out the socialist objectives of the Citizen Army. To have done so would have been no empty gesture, even in defeat. Had he issued his own platform making the call for a socialist Ireland he would at least have laid a foundation stone for future socialist movements. He would also have prevented political forces and individuals who represent the very antithesis of everything he stood for, from claiming his mantle.

Those who took part fought heroically and held out for a week against impossible odds. Connolly's courage under fire earned him the respect, not just of the men and women of the Citizen Army, but of the Volunteer ranks and even of some of the British officers.

After the rising came the reprisals. The main leaders were court-martialled and executed. Connolly was severely wounded and in no condition to face a court martial but General Maxwell, the British General in charge, insisted that it go ahead in the military hospital. Connolly was sentenced to death and taken in an ambulance to Kilmainham Gaol where he was shot on arrival. It was the revenge of the British ruling class – backed by their Irish counterparts – not just for the rising but for Connolly's lifetime of struggle against them.

The real tragedy of 1916 was clear to see just over one year later. In October 1917 the Bolsheviks led the Russian working class to power. The shock waves of revolution spread across Europe and beyond. Ireland too was convulsed by these events and a more favourable opportunity opened for the working class to take power than had existed at any time during Connolly's life.

But Connolly was dead and in his death the Irish working class were deprived of their foremost and outstanding leader. Connolly had not recognised the need to build a disciplined revolutionary party and so there was no force present to carry on his work. The movement ended not in revolution but in partition and defeat.

Our tribute to Connolly is not to join with the false eulogies that will drip hypocritically from the lips of the establishment, but to learn both from his accomplishments and his mistakes so that the experience of his life will assist the current generation to succeed in finally ridding the world of capitalism.

Common History, Common Struggle

Lessons from the 1960s
- when workers' unity &
socialism challenged
unionism & nationalism

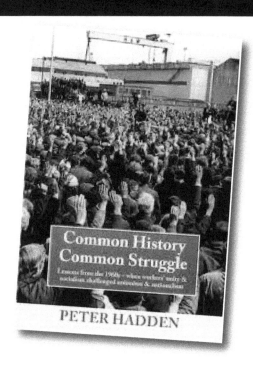

Limerick Soviet 1919

The revolt of the
Bottom Dog

By Dominic Haugh

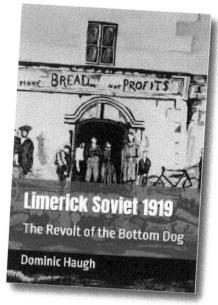

Workers' Power in Belfast

The story of the 1919 engineering strike

By Kevin Henry

Ireland's Lost Revolution

1916-1923 – The Working Class & the Struggle for Socialism

Introduction by Ruth Coppinger

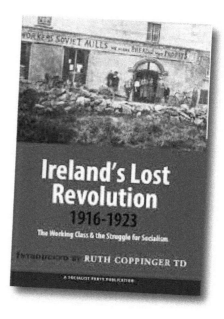

Join the Socialist Party

www.socialistparty.ie www.socialistpartyni.org

If you agree with the analysis outlined in this book, why not find out more about the ideas and actions of the Socialist Party?

NORTH: Text "JOIN" to 07821058319

SOUTH: Text "JOIN" to 0873141986

The Socialist Party is part International Socialist Alternative, an internation organisation of socialist groups based in over 30 countries. For more info: **internationalsocialist.n**

Lightning Source UK Ltd.
Milton Keynes UK
UKHW021121161120
373487UK00014B/1146